Fodor's

M000077672

los cabos

third edition

fodor's travel publications
new york · toronto · london · sydney · auckland
www.fodors.com

contents

maps

on the road with fodor's

A TRIP TAKES YOU OUT OF YOURSELF. Concerns of life at home completely disappear, driven away by more immediate thoughts—about, say, what marvels will beguile the next day, or where you'll have dinner. That's where Fodor's comes in. We make sure that you know all your options, so that you don't miss something that's around the next bend just because you didn't know it was there. Mindful that the best memories of your trip might have nothing to do with what you came to Los Cabos to see, we guide you to sights large and small all over the region. You might set out to bask in the Baja sun, but back at home you find yourself unable to forget the thrill of speeding along the dunes on an ATV. With Fodor's at your side, serendipitous discoveries are never far away.

About Our Writers

Our success in showing you every corner of Los Cabos is a credit to our extraordinary writers. Although there's no substitute for travel advice from a good friend who knows your style, our contributors are the next best thing—the kind of people you would poll for travel advice if you knew them.

Maribeth Mellin began covering Los Cabos for Fodor's in 1987. A journalist who has covered border issues from her home in the San Diego/Tijuana area, Maribeth has traveled the long road down the Baja Peninsula many times. Her writings on Mexico were recognized with the Pluma de Plata, Mexico's highest award for travel writing. She has authored books on Mexico, Costa Rica, Peru, Argentina, and other Latin American destinations.

You can rest assured that you're in good hands—and that no property mentioned in the book has paid to be included. Each has been selected strictly on its merits, as the best of its type in its price range.

HOW TO USE THIS BOOK

Icons and Symbols

★ Our special recommendations

🐣 Good for kids (rubber duck)

☞ Sends you to another section of the guide for more information

Numbers in white circles ③ and black circles ❸ that appear on the maps, in the margins, and within the tours correspond to one another.

For hotels, you can assume that all rooms have private baths, phones, TVs, and air-conditioning unless otherwise noted and that all hotels operate on the European Plan (with no meals) if we don't specify another meal plan. We always list a property's facilities but not whether you'll be charged extra to use them, so when pricing accommodations, do ask what's included. For restaurants, it's always a good idea to book ahead; we mention reservations only when they're essential or are not accepted. All restaurants we list are open daily for lunch and dinner unless stated otherwise; dress is mentioned only when men are required to wear a jacket or a jacket and tie. Look for an overview of local dining-out habits in the introduction of the Eating Out chapter.

Don't Forget to Write

Your experiences—positive and negative—matter to us. If we have missed or misstated something, we want to hear about it. We follow up on all suggestions. Contact the Los Cabos editor at editors@fodors.com or c/o Fodor's at 1745 Broadway, New York, NY 10019. And have a fabulous trip!

Tim Jarrell
Publisher

baja california sur

los cabos

The couple had returned to the "little village" where they had honeymooned 40 years earlier. Now they found themselves sitting amid a boisterous crowd at a beachside restaurant in Cabo San Lucas. They held hands and looked a little dismayed at the scantily clad couple dancing in the sand. Suddenly, she looked at him with a mischievous grin. "Shall we?" He smiled and replied, "Why not?" as they joined the gyrating couple to the applause of the thirtysomething crowd.

In This Chapter

By Joan Gonzalez

Revised by Maribeth Mellin

introducing los cabos

WHERE DESERT AND OCEAN COLLIDE, Los Cabos sits like a sun-splashed oasis that ends at El Arco, a dramatic stone arch. To appreciate Cabo's natural beauty, look east to the sparkling aquamarine waters of the Sea of Cortez and gaze west as a fiery-orange sun descends slowly into the pounding Pacific Ocean. At the tip of Mexico's Baja peninsula, 1,669 km (1,035 mi) south of Tijuana, Los Cabos is a remote hot spot for fun seekers and sun worshippers.

Los Cabos comprises three distinct areas: the pleasant, traditionally Mexican town of San José del Cabo; outrageous, action-packed Cabo San Lucas; and, connecting the two, the Corridor—a 33-km (20-mi) strip of golf courses and resorts set amid a desert landscape. The population of Los Cabos is said to be around 50,000, although unofficial estimates inflate it to 100,000, citing the growing number of Mexicans migrating from the mainland in search of jobs and the surge of part-time residents who have purchased vacation homes.

Shops and markets overflow with manufactured ceramics, weavings, embroidered clothing, silver jewelry, and exceptional folk art from Baja and mainland Mexico. In many hotels, traditional mariachi bands entertain as you dine on Mexican fare. Without these reminders, it would be easy to forget that Los Cabos is in Mexico, as American accents far outnumber Spanish on the streets. In addition to the tourist influx, full- and part-time residents from the United States and Canada buy condos, participate in time-shares, or lease villas—whatever it takes to prolong their stay in this sunny vacationland.

Los Cabos lays claim to more than 350 days of sunshine a year. Having a day's activity spoiled by rain is rare, except from August to November, when the occasional hurricane brings everything to a halt. The climate is dry and hot, tempered by low humidity and cool breezes off the Sea of Cortez. The hottest temperatures occur from June through September, the coolest from December through April—when a sweater or jacket is usually needed in the evenings.

But there's more to enjoy than perfect weather, lovely resorts, and scenery scalloped by the Sea of Cortez. Centuries of waves crashing against the shoreline have carved out sandy coves amid huge rock outcroppings, making them perfect for swimming, snorkeling, kayaking, and scuba diving.

Fishing is still the prime water sport, whether in *pangas* (small motorized skiffs) or luxury fishing yachts. Catch-and-release is encouraged, especially for marlin, which can range from 100 pounds to more than half a ton. Between January and late March, one of the most thrilling adventures is whale-watching: gray whales migrate from the Bering Strait to winter in Cabo's warm waters, where the females give birth.

There's a lot to do on land, too. Throughout Los Cabos, new golf courses are opening almost as fast as new hotels. Some are born from the drawing boards of such famous designers as Jack Nicklaus and Tom Weiskopf. You can also hike or bike through the Sierra de la Laguna mountain range, take ATV (all-terrain vehicle) trips along the beaches and into the desert, or hit the trails on horseback.

As that golden orb kisses the western horizon, life in Cabo is only just beginning. Set off on a sunset dinner cruise, dance barefoot at a beach party, or sample dusk-to-nearly-dawn nightlife in San Lucas—the party town that some have dubbed Cabo San Loco.

Baja Is Born

Los Cabos would not be a world apart today were it not for the gradual shifting of tectonic plates along the San Andreas fault, which extends north to San Francisco. The North Pacific and North American plates shifted over millions of years, creating an area where the Sea of Cortez could form. The sea slowly grew along the western side of mainland Mexico and extended north to the Colorado River. The plates gradually slid westward, forming the peninsula and the mountain ranges that create the dramatic landscape of the Baja California Peninsula.

Baja's earliest inhabitants likely crossed the Bering Strait between Asia and North American around 50,000 BC. When Spanish explorers first encountered the region, they mistakenly believed Baja was an island. Then in 1539 an expedition sent by Hernán Cortés discovered the mouth of the Colorado River and confirmed Baja to be a peninsula. They named the waterway El Mar de Cortés (Sea of Cortez) in honor of their leader.

THE MAKING OF LOS CABOS

Long before Spanish conquistadors arrived in the 16th century, the southern Baja peninsula was inhabited by the Guaycura people, who were divided between the Pericú and Guaycura tribes. Far less technologically developed than the indigenous peoples of mainland Mexico, the Guaycura were hunters and gatherers who lived simply in caves or crude shelters, wearing little or no clothing. The harsh environmental conditions of the southern peninsula and the constant search for food determined their lifestyle, and their isolation kept them unconcerned with building grand monuments. There are precious few signs of southern Baja's earliest inhabitants, save the chipped arrow points found in remote areas. Unlike tribes farther north, the Guaycura living around Los Cabos created little of Baja's famous rock art. Some rock paintings have been discovered in remote inland areas, but the majority of the peninsula's famous petroglyphs are in central Baja.

Spaniard Fortún Jiménez is credited with the first sighting of La Paz in what is now the state of Baja California Sur in early 1534, but Hernán Cortés is the officially recognized discoverer (May 1535). Juan Rodríguez Cabrillo explored the Pacific coastline from the tip of Baja to Santa Barbara in the mid-1500s, and his expedition team made it as far as Oregon. But the peninsula was not claimed by the Spaniards until 1663. The groundwork for the development of Los Cabos was really laid by Jesuit priests. Up to the time of their expulsion from Spain in 1768 by King Carlos III, the Jesuits had set up 17 missions north of Cabo San Lucas, including a small settlement in 1730 that was to become San José del Cabo. Nicolás Tamaral, a Jesuit priest, worked diligently to build up his mission, going into the mountains to find and convert the Pericú and other tribes; he is said to have baptized more than 1,000 Indians in his first year. Tamaral's efforts to convince the traditionally polygamous Pericú to become monogamous led to one of the largest uprisings in southern Baja. When Tamaral punished a Pericú leader for his sexual activity, the tribe revolted, killing and beheading Tamaral.

The Iglesia San José, across from the town's central plaza, was originally built in 1735, one year after Tamaral's death. The original church fell into ruins, and a new church was built on the site in the 1940s. A tile mosaic over the church entrance depicts Father Tamaral being dragged to his death. The Pericú and other indigenous groups were nearly wiped out by syphilis and smallpox, which had been introduced by waves of European settlers.

San José reached the 20th century as a successful settlement, largely due to its production of sugarcane, tomatoes, avocados, mangos, and other fruit, as well as cattle farming. At one time, more than 25,000 head of cattle roamed the countryside. From

1920 to 1930, a period known as the golden decade, large adobe homes were erected, Ford Motor cars rolled down the streets, and a dirt road was built connecting San José with Cabo San Lucas. Over the ensuing years, the town's prosperity gradually declined, due to new restrictions on shipping, bad management, and competition from other countries. San José was nearly bankrupt by the mid-1960s.

Cabo San Lucas was, for much of the 19th and early 20th centuries, just a laid-back little fishing village with few inhabitants. During World War II, pilots flying over Baja California Sur sighted large game fish in the waters around El Arco, and word of these fertile fishing grounds soon spread. In the mid-1950s, two prescient Baja aficionados constructed handsome fishing-lodge hotels with private airstrips in the Corridor. The Palmilla (rechristened the One&Only Palmilla) and Hotel Cabo San Lucas, overlooking the Sea of Cortez, remain two of the most impressive resorts in Los Cabos. By the mid-1960s the region had gained a reputation as one of the hottest fishing destinations in the world. A small building boom followed, attracting yacht owners and wealthy fishermen, including Hollywood celebrities Bing Crosby, Desi Arnaz, and John Wayne.

In the early 1970s, the Mexican government's tourism agency, Fonatur, acknowledged Los Cabos as a potential tourist destination. It began developing Cancún around the same time. Fonatur laid the infrastructure for Los Cabos in San José, building a hotel zone with paved streets and lighting and a 9-hole golf course. Entrepreneurs and developers saw more potential in Cabo San Lucas and the Corridor and began a building boom that has yet to end.

Preparations for the 2002 Asian Pacific Economic Conference (APEC), held in Los Cabos, included massive infrastructure improvements. A toll road was constructed between the airport and the Corridor, bridges over arroyos were built, and lines were put in for high-speed Internet access. As a result, Los Cabos has moved far into the 21st century, becoming perhaps the most modern resort area in Mexico.

PORTRAITS

THE PEOPLE

Most of the more than 75 million people living in Mexico today are descendants of native North Americans and Spaniards, with a few of African and East Asian descent whose ancestors were brought to the country as slaves. Los Cabos has its share of Spanish descendants (of the early conquistadores), but rounding out today's population are many transplants from mainland Mexico, the United States, Canada, and Europe.

Unlike other areas of Mexico with large indigenous populations—notably descendants of the Aztec, Maya, and Olmec, whose achievements can be seen in the ruins of their great stone cities—there is little evidence of the Pericú and Guaycura tribes that once inhabited Los Cabos. Some anthropologists say there are no descendants of Baja's original inhabitants in the area and that instead the ancestors of the ranchero families who populate the remote villages and towns came from northern California and the mainland or were descendants of the Spanish settlers, soldiers, and missionaries.

With its geographic separation and cultural isolation from mainland Mexico, Los Cabos differs in many respects from other Mexican resorts. The area has developed close ties to the United States (especially to California), and U.S. dollars are as common as pesos in the tourist areas. Costco and Wal-Mart have arrived, U.S. products line grocery store shelves, and U.S. investors are behind many of the large real estate developments. Many part-time and permanent residents come from California and the Pacific Northwest, as do the majority of tourists. Europeans have taken up residence here as well, investing in some of the most exciting restaurants and small hotels.

Huge numbers of workers are drawn to Los Cabos from mainland Mexico, eager to work in the construction and service industries. Unfortunately, this has caused concern about inadequate housing and facilities. Most workers live in neighborhoods tourists never see, along back streets and near Highway 19. It's clear why they come: there seems to be no unemployment in Los Cabos and the standard of living is higher than in many parts of the mainland. Begging is nearly nonexistent, and vendors selling jewelry, blankets, and hats are courteous and friendly. Mexican carpenters, bricklayers, housekeepers, waiters, lawyers, doctors, hoteliers, and other professionals seem to have unlimited prospects.

Most people who work in the tourist industry speak at least some English and are eager to learn more. In fact, the local language is basically Spanglish—a mix of English and Spanish that allows easy communication.

SPANISH GALLEONS & PIRATES

As a European settlement, Los Cabos had a raucous beginning. In 1578 Sir Francis Drake and his corsairs, backed by their English queen, were the first pirates to arrive in Los Cabos, finding its placid coves a perfect place to lay in wait for Spanish galleons. Sentinels watched for arriving ships from the highest point of the rock formation at El Arco, giving their comrades plenty of time to prepare for the attack. In the late 16th century, British, Dutch, and Chilean pirates used Chileno Bay and other coves along the Sea of Cortez as their base for preying on Spain's galleons sailing between Acapulco and the Philippines. They not only stole from the galleons but from each other, hiding the booty in caves along the coast and in the mountains. A 1,500-square-foot cave where the pirates were said to have buried some of their treasure is now included on nature walks around Hotel Cabo San Lucas.

Spain had established a regular trade route between Acapulco and the Philippines, carrying silver and gold from Mexico to Manila and bringing back silk and spices. San José del Cabo, at the time known as Aguada Segura ("place of safe water") and later as San Bernabe, was used as a shelter and provisioning point. The sailors, often sick with scurvy, could rest, pick up fresh water and food, and make any necessary repairs to their ships.

Local legend mentions a fierce English pirate called Cromwell who was said always to be favored by the winds. Ever since, whenever there is a favorable wind, it is called the *coromuel*, the local pronunciation of his name. According to the story, Cromwell and other pirates left behind a fortune in buried treasure in the hills behind Cabo San Lucas, but none has ever been found. It is said: "Only the 'coromuel' will tell you where the treasure is buried."

George Shelvocke, who came to the Los Cabos region in 1721, recorded cultural observations and published drawings of the Pericú, describing them as "tall, straight and well formed with large arms and black, thick, poorly cared for hair." He reported both sexes as having a good appearance with a dark copper skin color. Rather than portraying the Pericú as savage, Shelvocke reported that they appeared to be endowed with all imaginable humanity and might shame some other nations. "When one of us gave something edible to one of them in particular," he wrote, "he always divided it into as many parts as there were people around, and normally reserved the smallest part for himself."

WHERE DESERT MEETS OCEAN
The Sea of Cortez and the Pacific Ocean, which together form a semicircle at the tip of Los Cabos, are richer in flora and fauna than the desert that forms the landmass. Still, this relatively small region has a surprising mix of terrains and flora and fauna.

The Lay of the Land

In the late 1970s, the Mexican government slated the eastern tip of Baja Peninsula Sur for upscale tourism development and gave the area from San José del Cabo to Cabo San Lucas the name Los Cabos. New hotels and opulent resorts soon sprouted up between the two towns, and residents began calling this stretch of land "the tourism corridor," which soon was shortened to "the Corridor."

About 49 km (30 mi) south of the Tropic of Cancer, Mexico's Transpeninsular Highway (Highway 1) cuts southeast to the Sea of Cortez, defining the Los Cabos area. The region's mountainous topography is dominated by three ranges: La Laguna, which tops off at 6,857 feet above sea level; San Lazaro, at 5,217 feet; and La Trinidad, at 2,920 feet. Cool winter evenings and refreshing sea breezes keep the dry desert climate temperate. Annual rainfall of 5 to 10 inches hits between August and December, with the heaviest rains in September.

Sportfishing first put Los Cabos on the tourist map. With as many as 40,000 marlin and swordfish routinely hooked each year, the Mexican government was moved to establish strict rules governing the sport. Only one marlin, sailfish, or swordfish per fisherman a day is allowed, and anglers are strongly encouraged to return all billfish to the sea.

But the wealth of marine life goes far beyond world-record game fish. Included among the more than 850 species of fish swimming these waters are black codfish, bonito, dogfish, dorado, flounder, mackerel, rooster fish, sardines, sea bass, shark, small anchovy, tuna, and wahoo. Many varieties of mollusks and crustaceans, such as squid, clams, mussels, snail, lobster, fiddler crab, and shrimp, also live below the surface.

Fifty-foot gray whales migrate here each January, giving birth and then heading back north to the Bering Strait through early April. Colonies of seals and sea lions can be seen sunning themselves on the rocks around El Arco, one of the only "land's ends" in the world.

Leatherback turtles, the only sea turtles without a hard shell, come ashore between November and February. More than 100 of these large reptiles (some as long as 8 feet and topping 1,200 lbs) lumber up beaches along the Corridor to scoop out a hole in the sand, where they drop their eggs during the night. Each turtle delivers about 100 eggs, which drop two or three at a time every 4 to 10 seconds. The mother then returns to the sea to follow her migratory path, often swimming as far away as Japan. When eggs hatch (about 56 days later), the hatchlings scramble to the sea. Many are snatched up by birds. Those that survive may return 20 or 30 years later to lay their eggs on the same beach.

In addition to the leatherback, four other species are found in Baja California: the green turtle, hawksbill, loggerhead, and olive ridley. A Los Cabos–based organization, Associatión Subcalifornia de Proteccional Medio Ambiente y la Tortuga Marina (ASUPMATOMA; Association for the Protection of the Environment and the Marine Turtle in Southern Baja), raises awareness about these endangered creatures. To get involved, consult the ASUPMATOMA Web site at www.mexonline.com/tortuga.htm.

On trail hikes, you can walk through dry riverbeds at sea level up to mountains that peak near 7,000 feet to see cactus, tropical palms, and pine and oak trees growing in the same forest. Active hot springs and natural freshwater springs in the mountains disappear underground by the time they reach the foothills. Among the none-too-glamorous land fauna are coyote, wild sheep, badgers, gophers, California hare, and rice rats.

Almost half the 250 species of birds identified in Los Cabos are seacoast or open-sea birds; a small group are found in the high mountains. Species include the red-tailed hawk, black-tailed gnatcatcher, caspian tern, roadrunner, frigate bird, brown pelican, gila woodpecker, turkey vulture, osprey, quail, common ground and white-winged dove, cardinal, verdin, common yellow throat warbler, coot, and lesser nighthawk.

Nearly 3,000 plant species have been identified in Baja California, with almost 40% growing in the Los Cabos area. Of these, 275 are native to the region and found mostly on the dry and rocky hillsides. Despite an arid desert climate, Los Cabos has diverse soil types that support three general groups of vegetation: desert (mainly cacti); crops; and fruit trees. Among the 60 identified species of cacti are the plentiful cardon, said to cure toothaches and heal wounds; the pitahaya, whose fruit was a main staple of the Pericú Indians; and the giant, carrotlike cirio, native only to Baja California and Sonora. Other cactus varieties include the cholla, garambullo, palo adan, yucca, valida, and ocotillo. Common crops include strawberries, lettuces, melons, cucumbers, zucchini, and tomatoes. Mango and citrus trees, papaya, and coconut thrive near water sources, such as the San José River.

A TASTE OF LOS CABOS

For many years, it was impossible to get authentic Mexican fare in Los Cabos. Simple street stands and cafés served basic tacos, burritos, and grilled fish, along with burgers, stringy steaks, and basic pasta dishes. But the increase in tourism brought an increased demand for high-quality cuisine. Restaurants now serve authentic Mexican dishes, along with French, Spanish, Italian, Californian, Japanese, and Thai cuisine. A Baja cuisine based on fresh seafood and produce from local farms is emerging, and chefs are creating exciting combinations of Mexican and international recipes and seasonings.

Following the lead of other regions of Mexico, Los Cabos is developing individual specialties, using locally grown and raised ingredients and recipes handed down through generations. Originally, southern Baja had very few crops, but early settlers soon found pockets of fertile areas along rivers and underground springs. Many medicinal and culinary herbs are found in the mountains, and small towns such as Miraflores and Santiago cultivate some of the herbs and vegetables for Los Cabos restaurants. The road along the Pacific coast between Cabo San Lucas and Todos Santos is lined with commercial farms raising vegetables for export and for local markets and restaurants.

What Los Cabos has always had in abundance is seafood. From sea bass to tuna, mussels to squid, the fruits of the sea offer Los Cabos chefs a rich selection of ingredients for their culinary works of art. Some of the tastiest dishes are seafood soups, made with octopus, shrimp, fish, or crab. Fresh Pacific lobster is typically served simply with a butter sauce or in a salad with fresh greens. Homegrown terra fare includes local beef and pork that's been marinated and often grilled or barbecued. Most of the meat served in better restaurants is imported from Sonora on the mainland or from the United States.

As the area's popularity grows, the dining-out experience is expanding to beyond just the food, with the restaurants themselves often part of the attraction. Many of San José de Cabo's eateries are in restored 19th-century adobe houses, where you can dine indoors surrounded by original art or outside amid fountains and tropical gardens in a lovely courtyard—as at **DAMIANA** and **TEQUILA**. Adding to the international scene downtown is **BAAN THAI**, whose chef, a native of Thailand, prepares authentic dishes from his homeland.

The more lively town of Cabo San Lucas has some traditional restaurants, but eating out is more often an eclectic experience. For authentic Mexican home cooking, **MI CASA,** alongside Plaza

San Lucas, is highly regarded for its regional dishes, including the *chile en nogada*, a meat-stuffed pepper topped with walnut sauce and pomegranate seeds. **PANCHO'S** is known for its *huevos rancheros* (fried eggs on a tortilla and topped with salsa), **RISTORANTE DA GIORGIO** dishes out superb Italian fare, and **NICK-SAN** is noted for its outstanding sushi. The **OFFICE** on Playa Médano is the place for barefoot dining and beachside action.

Surprisingly, some of the best restaurants are in hotels. In 2004, Chicago celebrity-chef Charlie Trotter opened **C,** a chic contemporary dining room at the One&Only Palmilla resort. In downtown San José, the European-style boutique hotel Casa Natalia houses **MI COCINA,** where French owner Loïc Tenoux and his wife Nathalie (from Luxembourg) bring their European training to traditional Mexican dishes. Gourmands should not miss dining at The Restaurant at **LAS VENTANAS AL PARAÍSO** hotel. It's a splurge, but the breads alone are worth it. Groups can book the wine-cellar dining room.

It was early morning when the sound of tinkling bells coaxed the sleepy couple from their bed. Stepping onto their patio overlooking the beach, they saw an old man leading a string of horses, each with a bell around its neck. He brought them around to a shady spot, where he waited until the sun was high in the sky and vacationers came to rent a mount for a slow canter through the surf.

In This Chapter

By Joan Gonzalez

Revised by Maribeth Mellin

perfect days

THERE IS NO SINGLE RECIPE for a perfect day in Los Cabos. Variations abound, depending on your taste and how active you want—or don't want—to be. But whether you spend your entire trip on the beach or decide to hop from town to town without missing a sight or boutique, Los Cabos delivers.

A PERFECT DAY AT THE BEACH

A perfect day on a Los Cabos beach may require only three things: wine, bread, and Gatorade—a bit of the romantic along with the practical. To keep your memories of the day perfect, add sunscreen, sunglasses, and a hat. For a small deposit, many hotels provide beach towels, coolers, and umbrellas, or you can rent these and other convenience items from **TRADER DICK'S** (Hwy. 1, Km 29, tel. 624/142–2989), just west of the La Jolla de los Cabos Resort near the Costa Azul beach. Dicks also fixes good box lunches. In winter, bring a sweatshirt or sweater to the beach.

To get to the most pristine beaches along the Sea of Cortez, head east out of San José del Cabo by car. At the corner of Boulevard Mijares and Calle Benito Juárez in San José, turn east at the sign marked PUEBLO LA PLAYA. The paved street soon becomes a dirt road that leads to the small fishing villages of **LA PLAYA** (The Beach) and **LA PLAYITA** (The Little Beach), about 1½ km (½ mi) from San José. As of this writing, construction of a marina resort complex is underway here; watch for road detours.

From La Playita, drive 60 km (37 mi) up the coast to the ecological reserve **CABO PULMO,** home of Baja Sur's largest coral reef. Water depths range from 15 feet to 130 feet, and it seems Mother Nature created it just for divers, snorkelers, and swimmers. Tropical fish, rays, and other colorful marine life dart along the reef and among the many shipwrecks. If you plan to scuba dive, contact **CABO PULMO RESORT** (tel. 562/366-0398, 888/997-8566 in the U.S. [answered at Cabo Pulmo], www. cabopulmo.net). When hunger pangs call, stroll up the beach from Cabo Pulmo to **TITO'S** for a fish taco and an ice-cold *cerveza* (beer).

Try to get back to La Playa by late afternoon to avoid driving the East Cape's dirt road at night. After your hard work worshipping sun and surf, reward yourself with some fresh seafood and a frozen margarita at **BUZZARD'S BAR AND GRILL** right near the beach just north of La Playa. San José is only 10 minutes away.

A PERFECT PLAY DAY

From the Cabo San Lucas marina, board one of the glass-bottom boats that depart regularly for dramatic **EL ARCO** (the Arch) and **PLAYA DEL AMOR** (Lover's Beach), the sandy stretch in El Arco's shadow. Or head out in a kayak or tour boat from Playa Médano. The boat ride is half the fun, especially if you cruise by the sea lion colony on the rocks near the arch. The Sea of Cortez and the Pacific Ocean, which merge here, have been compared to the people of San Lucas: *cortés* (courteous) and *pacífico* (gentle). Swim and snorkel only on the Sea of Cortez side, though; the Pacific side is too rough.

There's usually a vendor or two selling water and cold drinks on the beach, but nothing more. Bring along lots of drinking water, snacks, sunscreen, and a towel. The snorkeling is usually good around the rocks edging the sand. After a few hours on the beach, board the next boat back to the marina or paddle back to

Sensational Sunsets

Cabo's brilliant sunsets are best viewed from the Pacific side of Baja's tip. The Finisterra's Whale Watcher Bar and the Solmar's palapa (palm thatch) bar have long been favorite perches for ocean lovers any time of day. As gold and rose tint the sky, all eyes turn westward to the long, nearly empty beach and the endless expanse of natural scenery. Most sunset cruise boats glide past the land-bound onlookers. If you want to be part of the scenery, board the Pirate Cruise or La Princesa.

On the Sea of Cortez side of the tip, El Arco, Cabo's famous Arch, stands out against the sunset's glow. Claim one of the cliff-top tables at Ristorante Da Giorgio for spectacular panoramas, or join the revelers praising the fading light at one of Playa Médano's beach bars. One of the best ways to enjoy the sunset in San José del Cabo is to go horseback riding on the beach. This can be arranged at most of the hotels.

shore. This is a good time to settle in for a leisurely lunch on **PLAYA MÉDANO.** The outdoor eateries along this sandy stretch are as casual and colorful as their names. Order a cold drink and a big plate of tacos or grilled fish at **BILLYGAN'S ISLAND,** the **OFFICE,** or **MANGO DECK.**

Once you're reenergized, try parasailing, surfing, or riding a WaveRunner at Playa Médano. Activity centers on the sand rent every imaginable beach toy, along with umbrellas and lounge chairs. Head for your hotel in mid-afternoon and change into pants for a sunset horseback ride on the beach. Both **RED ROSE RIDING STABLES** and **CUADRA SAN FRANCISCO** have horses for all levels of riders. After the sun sets, dine at one of San Lucas's rock-and-roll hangouts.

A PERFECT DAY OF SIGHTSEEING

For first-timers trying to get a feel for the area, it's a good idea to take an organized sightseeing tour at the beginning of the vacation. If you're ready to set out on your own, start your tour at **LA FÁBRICA DE VIDRIO SOPLADO** (Blown-Glass Factory)—a bit hard to find if you're driving yourself. First head toward San José on Avenida Cárdenas, which turns into Highway 1. Turn left at the stoplight and signs for the bypass to Todos Santos; then look for signs to the factory. The factory is in an industrial area two blocks northwest of Highway 1. Most taxi drivers know the way and charge about $8 from Cabo San Lucas. At the factory, you can watch artisans, who produce more than 450 pieces a day, use a process that has changed little since it was first developed some 4,000 years ago. The on-site store sells many of these pieces. Admission is free, but you can drop a donation in the bowl near the artisans.

From the factory, head east on Highway 1 for the 20-minute drive to San José del Cabo. In San José, stop for an authentic, inexpensive Mexican lunch at **LA CENADURÍA** (Av. Zaragoza and Plaza Mijares). Park at the south end of Boulevard Mijares around the Tropicana restaurant, since traffic tends to get very congested in the next few blocks. Take your time wandering through the shops on Mijares, and then settle in at a table in the restaurant's courtyard. Try the mixed-seafood specialty Las Cazuelas, which is cooked in a clay pot.

After lunch, stroll across the street to the plaza in front of the **IGLESIA SAN JOSÉ** (mission church) and join the locals in this tree-shaded square. Everything in San José moves at a slow pace, so don't feel guilty if all you feel like doing is wandering in and out of shops and art galleries.

Return to your hotel for dinner or try **MI COCINA** (☎ 624/142–5100; reservations essential), an outdoor restaurant at the Casa Natalia hotel (at the north end of Boulevard Mijares). European dishes with a Mexican flair are served amid dramatic lighting, cascading waterfalls, and flaming braziers.

A PERFECT DAY IN TODOS SANTOS

For a respite from the bustling crowds of Los Cabos, head 45 minutes north of San Lucas along Highway 19 to this small, laid-back town. The Águila bus that leaves the San Lucas terminal every two hours is more comfortable and less expensive than trips offered by tour operators—though a cab to the bus station can cost $8 from downtown San Lucas. No announcements are made, so get off when the bus stops at **PILAR'S FRESH FISH TACOS,** or you'll wind up in La Paz. Cross the street and walk up Avenida Zaragoza to Benito Juárez.

Continue along Benito Juárez to the gorgeously restored **HOTEL CALIFORNIA.** Turn left at the corner of Calle Máquez de León to see the **MISIÓN DE NUESTRA SEÑORA DEL PILAR** (Mission of Our Lady of Pilar). Off to the right, on Calle Centenario, is the **CAFÉ SANTA FÉ,** one of the first buildings in Todos Santos to be renovated, starting a trend that revived the area. The café has a beautiful garden and serves organic dishes. Along any street, explore interesting cafés, shops, and galleries. Stop by **EL TECOLOTE BOOKSTORE,** on the corner of Benito Juárez and Calle Hidalgo, for a free copy of El Calendario de Todos Santos, with articles on local artists and reviews of restaurants, shops, and galleries.

To take the bus back to Los Cabos, walk east toward the ocean on Benito Juárez to Avenida Zaragoza, and turn left. Walk one block and wait on the corner in front of the park. You can pay ($9) on board in pesos or dollars. Take a taxi back to your hotel from the San Lucas station.

After a long night of barhopping and dancing, the couple had one thing on their minds—tacos. Turning off the main street, they slid into a 24-hour taquería and scanned a bible of choices. Tired and a little bleary-eyed, it took them a few minutes: beef, chicken, shrimp, sea bass? Cactus flower, squash blossom, haban-what? A little salsa, a drizzle of chili sauce, and their sizzlin' night just got hotter.

In This Chapter

Revised by Maribeth Mellin

eating out

FROM ELEGANT DINING ROOMS TO CASUAL SEAFOOD CAFÉS, Los Cabos serves up French, Italian, Japanese, Thai, vegetarian, kosher, and, of course, Mexican cuisine. Unfortunately, most restaurants try to please everyone and overcome fierce competition by offering similar menus with often mediocre results. But a few chefs and restaurateurs have found their niches and their audiences. The food scene changes quickly, and a place that shines one month may be only satisfactory the next. It's always a good idea to ask fellow travelers about their dining experiences.

Seafood is the truly local cuisine. Fresh catches that land on area menus include dorado (mahimahi), *lenguado* (halibut), *cabrilla* (sea bass), *jurel* (yellowtail), and marlin. Native lobster, shrimp, and octopus are particularly good. Fish grilled over a wood fire is perhaps the most indigenous dish. The most popular may be the *taco de pescado* (fish taco), which has many variations but is traditionally a deep-fried fillet wrapped in a handmade corn tortilla, served with shredded cabbage, cilantro, and sauces. Beef and pork, commonly served grilled and marinated, are also quite good. Many restaurants import their steak, lamb, duck, and quail from Sonora, Mexico's prime pastureland.

In San José, several international chefs prepare excellent Continental, Asian, and Mexican dishes in lovely restaurants. The Corridor is the place to go for exceptional hotel restaurants. San Lucas has comfort food covered, with franchise eateries from Domino's to Carlos 'n' Charlie's to Ruth's Chris Steak House.

PRICES

Restaurants in Los Cabos tend to be pricey, even by U.S. standards. Some places add a 15% service charge to the bill and some add a fee for credit-card usage. If you wander off the beaten path—often only a few blocks from the touristy areas— you can find inexpensive, authentic Mexican fare (though still more expensive than elsewhere in Mexico). The restaurants we list are the cream of the crop in each price category.

CATEGORY	COST*
$$$$	over $30
$$$	$20–$30
$$	$10–$20
$	$5–$10
¢	under $5

*All prices are per person for a main course at dinner.

HOW & WHEN

Restaurants generally don't stay open late; if you arrive after 10 PM, you're taking your chances. Most are open year-round and only close one night a week, typically Sunday or Monday. Unless otherwise noted, the restaurants listed in this guide are open daily for lunch and dinner. In this chapter, reservations are mentioned only when they're essential, but it's a good idea to make reservations everywhere during high season. You may have to wait a half hour or so at the popular restaurants that don't take reservations. Dress is casual. Polo shirts and nice slacks are fine even in the most upscale places; shirts and shoes (or sandals) are a must except on the beach.

SAN JOSÉ DEL CABO

$$–$$$ **EL CHILAR.** The fine selection of Mexican wines and tequilas suits
★ the stylish Mexican menu at this small restaurant, decorated with bright orange walls and murals of the Virgin of Guadalupe. In his open kitchen, chef Armando Montaño uses chilies from all over

Mexico to enhance traditional and Continental dishes (without heating up the spice), coating rack of lamb with ancho chile and perking up lobster bisque with smoky *chiles guajillos*. *Calle Juárez at Morelos, tel. 624/142–2544. No credit cards. Closed Sun., no lunch.*

$$–$$$ **MI COCINA.** Bring a special someone to this charming torch-lit
★ terrace, where the widely spaced tables will keep your sweet nothings from prying ears. Chef Loïc Tenoux is always playing with ingredients, creating eclectic nibbles like a *pizzetta* with Oaxacan cheese or a divine fried Camembert (you can stop in for tapas and tequila martinis if you don't want a complete meal). For the full dinner experience, start with cilantro pesto lobster salad, and move on to rack of lamb with couscous and asparagus—all unusual for the area. Even filet mignon takes a new twist with black truffle olive oil on the twice-baked potato. Keep an eye out for celebrities here. *Casa Natalia, Blvd. Mijares 4, tel. 624/142–5100. AE, MC, V. No lunch.*

$$–$$$ **LA PANGA.** With brick walls enclosing the spacious yet cozy dining room, this hotel-zone restaurant is a winner. The menu is a seafood lover's dream, starting with Baja mussels in chardonnay sauce or an Alaskan king crab burrito with mango relish. Hearty main courses vying for your attention include prawns over gruyère cheese risotto and panfried salmon with black bean ragout. Save room for the mango-and-coconut mousse cake. *Paseo Malecón at Bahía de Palmas, tel. 624/142–4041. AE, MC, V.*

$–$$$ **DAMIANA.** Bougainvillea-wrapped pines shade wrought-iron
★ tables, and pink adobe walls glow in the candlelight at this small hacienda tucked beside the plaza. Start with fiery oysters diablo; then move on to the tender chateaubriand, charbroiled lobster, or the restaurant's signature shrimp steak, made with ground shrimp. This place is so relaxing, you might want to linger well into the night. *Blvd. Mijares 8, tel. 624/142–0499. AE, MC, V.*

$–$$$ **TEQUILA RESTAURANTE.** An old adobe home sets the stage for
★ a classy dining experience. A lengthy tequila list gives you a chance to savor the finer brands of Mexico's national drink, and

san josé del cabo dining

El Ahorcado
Taqueria, 10

Baan Thai, 7

Baja Natural, 9

Buzzard's
Bar & Grill, 1

La Cenaduría, 4

El Chilar, 2

Damiana, 5

Fandango, 8

Mi Cocina, 6

La Panga, 11

Tequila
Restaurante, 3

the menu challenges you to decide between excellent regional dishes and innovative Pacific Rim spring rolls, salads, and seafood with mango, ginger, and citrus sauces. Take your time and sample all you can. *Manuel Doblado s/n, tel. 624/142–1155. AE.*

$$ FANDANGO. ★ The menu offerings are ever-changing at this quirky restaurant with contemporary cuisine. You can usually get sweet-potato fritters, Greek salad, grilled veggies, fresh baby green beans with chilies and toasted almonds, and seared salmon, sea bass, or tuna with shiitake fried rice—as well as whatever produce sparks the chef's imagination. A festive mural and colorful Chinese umbrellas contrast with the serene candlelit patio. *Obregón 19, at Morelos, tel. 624/142–2226. MC, V. Closed Sun.*

$–$$ BAAN THAI. ★ An Asian furniture importer and a Thai chef teamed up to create an authentic Thai restaurant full of visual and culinary delights. Antiques fill the formal dining room, and the relaxing patio has a murmuring fountain and Thai black bamboo furniture. Delicious, reasonably priced dishes are made with ingredients imported from Thailand. *Tom Kha Gai* (spicy chicken in coconut milk with lemongrass and mushrooms) and *Kao Pad Sap Pa Ros* (fried rice with shrimp and cashew nuts served in a half pineapple) are two highlights. *Morelos and Obregón (across from El Encanto Inn), tel. 624/142–3344. AE, MC, V. Closed Sun.*

$–$$ BUZZARD'S BAR & GRILL. ★ Fronted by miles of secluded beach, this casual seaside cantina gets rave reviews from locals who drive out to escape the Los Cabos madness. Former Southern California restaurant owners Denny and Judie Jones serve up hefty steaks, seafood dinners, and burgers, plus a Sunday breakfast that's a big hit. To get here, turn off Boulevard Mijares at the signs for La Playa and follow the road up the hill past La Playa; it's about 10 minutes from San José in the Laguna Hills neighborhood. *Old East Cape Road, tel. 702/255–0630 in the U.S. No credit cards.*

$–$$ LA CENADURÍA. Dine on the airy rooftop overlooking the pretty town square or one level down under a large *palapa* (palm-thatch)

Dining In

Eating every meal in a Los Cabos restaurant can devour your dollars quickly. Most food and liquor is shipped from the mainland or imported from the United States, resulting in premium prices. Many hotel rooms have small refrigerators and coffeemakers; some have microwaves, too. By stocking up on groceries you can save your money for splurges.

Supermarkets such as Cabo San Lucas's **ARAMBURO** (Av. Cárdenas across from Hard Rock Cafe, tel. 624/143–1450), open 7 AM–11 PM, and neighborhood markets sell the basics for quick meals. Watch out for the prices on imported goods—a box of imported cereal can cost $5 or more. Stick with Mexican brands. Prices are lower at **ISSSTE** (Av. de la Juventud and Morelos, tel. 624/143–4658) in Cabo San Lucas. It's open 8–8. Inventory is limited, however, and no meat or produce is sold. A good strategy is to get what you can at ISSSTE, then tap the smaller markets away from touristy areas. At **COSTCO** (Hwy. 1, Km 4.5, tel. 624/146–7180), members can stock up on inexpensive supplies. Liquor stores are generally less expensive than supermarkets and stay open until 11 PM (earlier on Sunday).

roof amid walls painted teal, purple, yellow, and orange. Included on the typical Sinaloan menu are *enmoladas* (enchiladas in a six-chili mole sauce) and homemade tamales. The Mexican sampler—tacos, quesadillas, chiles rellenos, and an enchilada—is an excellent deal. For dessert, try a platter of pumpkin, cactus, caramel, and sesame candies. Av. Zaragoza 10 at Plaza Principal, tel. 624/148–7117. No credit cards.

¢–$ **EL AHORCADO TAQUERÍA.** By day it looks like a hole-in-the-
★ wall, but by night this open-air eatery comes to life. It's one of the few restaurants in town open late, and both tourists and locals ensure that it stays packed until closing, usually around 3 AM. Hanging from the walls and rafters is a mishmash of old pots, baskets, antique irons, and sombreros with yellow lightbulbs. Tacos and enchiladas come with such tasty fillers as *flor de calabaza*

(squash blossom), *nopales* (cactus flower), and *rajas* (poblano chilies). It's a bit outside the town center, so you need to drive or take a taxi. *Paseo Pescadores and Marinos, tel. 624/148–2437. No credit cards. Closed Mon.*

¢ **BAJA NATURAL.** This popular juice and sandwich shop has a convenient take-a-break location near the highway. Cool off with one of dozens of fresh-fruit smoothies and juices, shakes, and powerdrinks, or refuel with a hamburger, hot dog, or veggie burger. *Manuel Doblado at Hwy. 1, tel. 624/142–3105. No credit cards. Closed Sun.*

THE CORRIDOR
With a few exceptions, dining in the Corridor is restricted to hotel restaurants.

$$$–$$$$ **C.** Chicago chef Charlie Trotter has extended his empire to Mexico
★ with this chic contemporary restaurant at the One&Only Palmilla resort. Have a drink at the adjacent open-air bar, overlooking the rocky coastline and open sea, before strolling past the cylindrical aquariums that divide the open kitchen from the L.A.-urbane dining room. Trotter's daily-changing menu emphasizes vegetables that rarely appear in Cabo—you might find salsify, wax beans, or turnips. You might also encounter such first-rate inventions as tuna with crispy polenta, grouper with jasmine rice and napa cabbage, or squab with butternut squash risotto. *One&Only Palmilla, Hwy. 1, Km. 7.5, tel. 624/146–7000. Reservations essential. AE, MC, V. No lunch.*

$$$–$$$$ **PITAHAYAS.** This elegant restaurant occupies a lovely niche above
★ the beach at Cabo del Sol. The Pacific Rim menu blends Thai, Polynesian, and Chinese influences in unusual recipes. Lobster might have a vanilla bean sauce, octopus turns up in a spicy salad, and the catch of the day comes with a refreshing mango relish. Soft live jazz plays in the background, adding to the seductive setting. Reservations are recommended. *Hwy. 1, Km 10, tel. 624/145–8010. AE, MC, V.*

the corridor dining

C., 2
Enrique's
Steak & Lobster
House, 5
Pitahayas, 3
Ristorante
Da Giorgio, 4
Zippers, 1

$$–$$$ RISTORANTE DA GIORGIO. Tables set along the cliffs have full-
★ on views of El Arco—particularly dramatic during the sunset
cocktail hour. The first-rate modern Italian fare in the handsome
candlelit dining room lives up to the setting as well. Try the lobster
pasta, the crab with garlic and olive oil, or the pasta with anchovies
and capers. Totally romantic, this is definitely a good spot for a
special night out. *Hwy. 1, Km 5, at Misiones del Cabo, tel. 624/145–
8160. Reservations essential for dinner. MC, V.*

$–$$ ENRIQUE'S STEAK & LOBSTER HOUSE. Scores of tourists and
locals alike come here for one of the best deals around—the
$9.95 Gone Loco special. Choose two of six options—shrimp,
lobster, steak, sea bass, chicken, or ribs—accompanied by soup
or salad, garlic bread, rice, and steamed vegetables. The regular
menu includes quail with plum sauce and T-bone steak. Though
spacious, the bilevel restaurant feels intimate under a large
palapa roof and soft lighting. Dance bands play every evening.
Hwy. 1, Km 4.5, tel. 624/143–0969. MC, V.

$–$$ ZIPPERS. Home of the surfing crowd and those who like a bit of
sand in their burgers, this casual palapa-roof restaurant sits on
Costa Azul beach just south of San José. Burgers, ribs, and chicken
are all decent, but it's the crowd that makes the place fun. Sporting
events are shown on large TVs at the bar. *Hwy. 1, Km 18.5, no phone.
No credit cards.*

CABO SAN LUCAS

$$$–$$$$ LORENZILLO'S. Gleaming hardwood floors and polished brass
give a nautical flair to this upstairs dining room where fresh
lobster is king. Lorenzillo's has long been a fixture in Cancún, where
lobster is raised on the company's farm. That Caribbean lobster
is shipped to Los Cabos and served 12 different ways (the simpler
preparations—steamed or grilled with lots of melted butter—are
the best). It's a major splurge—a two-pounder served with spinach
puree and linguine or potato will set you back over $50—though
other options, perhaps coconut shrimp or beef medallions, are

cabo san lucas dining

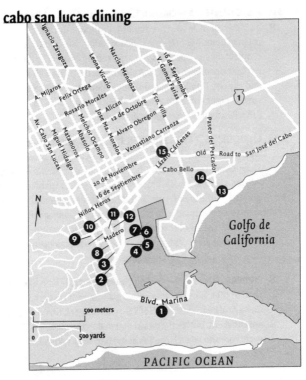

more moderately priced. *Cárdenas at the Marina, tel. 624/105–0212. AE, MC, V.*

$$–$$$ CAPO SAN GIOVANNIS. The sound of sauces simmering in the open kitchen blends with strains of opera at this intimate Italian restaurant. Owner Gianfranco Zappata, and his wife and master pastry chef, Antonella, perform a culinary concert that keeps you coming back for encores. Try their green salad with lobster chunks, cioppino Calabrese, spaghetti with crab, and *mela* (an apple-and-nut pastry topped with caramel). For a romantic touch, dine on the starlit back patio. There's a 10% discount for cash. *Guerrero at Av. Cárdenas, tel. 624/143–0593. MC, V. Closed Mon.*

$$–$$$ EDITH'S CAFÉ. Caesar salad and flambéed crepes are served table-side at this small café, where dinners are accompanied by Mexican trios and soft jazz. Even the simplest quesadilla is enhanced by Oaxacan cheese and homemade tortillas, and the meat and fish dishes are creative, with unusual chili or tropical fruit sauces. Early evenings sometimes bustle with families, so dine later if you're looking for romance. *Paseo del Pescador near Playa Médano, tel. 624/143–0801. MC, V.*

$$–$$$ EL GALEÓN. Considered by some the most distinguished dining room in town, El Galeón serves traditional Italian, Mexican, and American fare. Dishes are expertly prepared, with an emphasis on thick, tender cuts of beef. The choice seats look out to the marina, and the heavy wooden furnishings and white linens lend a sense of formality. Stop into the piano bar for a late-night brandy. *Across from marina by the road to Finisterra Hotel, tel. 624/143–0443. AE, MC, V.*

$$–$$$ MI CASA. One of the best places for regional Mexican cuisine is this eye-catching restaurant opposite the main plaza; it's in a cobalt-blue building painted with a burro mural. Fresh tuna and dorado are served with tomatillo salsa or Yucatecan achiote (ground annatto seed). The *chile en nogada* (a meat-stuffed pepper topped with walnut sauce and pomegranate seeds) is a classic.

The terraced back courtyard is especially seductive at night, illuminated by candles and moonlight. The owners also run Peacock's and Mi Casa del Mar, which are worth a meal stop, too. *Av. Cabo San Lucas, tel. 624/143–1933. MC, V. No lunch Sun.*

$$–$$$ PANCHO'S. Nearly 500 brands of tequila, delicious seafood, and regional Mexican specialties make this festive place a favorite among locals in the know. Take advantage of owner John Bragg's encyclopedic knowledge of tequila and sample a few varieties. Try tortilla soup, chiles rellenos, stuffed bacon-wrapped shrimp, or the reasonably-priced breakfasts. Oaxacan tablecloths, murals, painted chairs, and streamers add to the fun. *Hidalgo between Zapata and Serdan, tel. 624/143–0973. AE, MC, V.*

$$–$$$ SANCHO PANZA. ★ The sophisticated menu, furnishings, and wine list make this small bistro an excellent spot for dining, drinking, and enjoying live jazz. Try the steamed mussels, osso buco, and chile relleno stuffed with *huitlacoche* (a mushroom-like fungus grown on corn). The menu changes constantly, as do both the art in the Daliesque bar and the extraordinary selection of imported wines. The restaurant hosts wine and tequila tastings and other special events. Check out the menu and events at the start of your stay—you may come back repeatedly. *Blvd. Marina behind KFC and Plaza Las Glorias, tel. 624/143–3212. AE, MC, V.*

$$–$$$ SEA QUEEN. The dining room is enormous, but the service is attentive at this standout seafood restaurant. Fresh sushi is prepared in view of the diners, and the chef adds regional flair to his fish dishes with poblano, guajillo, or chipotle chilies. The Mexican combo plate, New York steak, or Thai chicken salad should satisfy those who've had their fill of seafood. *Av. Cabo San Lucas at Blvd. Marina, tel. 624/144–4731. MC, V.*

$–$$$ NICK SAN. ★ A creative fusion of Japanese and Mexican cuisines distinguishes the extensive menu here. How about panfried curry-flavor oysters with cucumber sauce, lobster and vegetable tempura, or a platter of rosy pink sashimi? The lunch menu includes noodle and curry dishes. Watch the chefs at work in the open kitchen or at the handsome mahogany sushi bar, where some of the best sushi in Cabo is deftly prepared. *Blvd. Marina, next to Plaza Las Glorias, tel. 624/143–4484. MC, V.*

$–$$ FISH HOUSE. Walk up the stairs to this glassed-in terrace restaurant and leave the noisy bars and marina action behind. Courteous waters bustle between tables spread with green cloths, serving tuna carpaccio, scallop ceviche, and spicy calamari salad. Fried chicken and other meat dishes are available for dedicated carnivores, but why not try dorado or snapper fresh from the sea? *Blvd. Marina at Plaza de la Danza, tel. 624/144–4501. MC, V.*

$–$$ MARISQUERÍA MAZATLÁN. The crowds of locals lunching at this
★ simple restaurant are a good sign—as are the huge glasses packed with shrimp, ceviche, and other seafood cocktails. You can dine inexpensively on wonderful seafood soup, or spend a bit more for tender *pulpo ajillo* (marinated octopus with garlic, chilies, onion, and celery). It's hard to choose among oysters, blue crab, 12 shrimp preparations, or whole grilled snapper. *Mendoza at 16 Septiembre, tel. 624/143–8565. MC, V.*

$–$$ MISIONES DE KINO. You may feel like you've discovered a well-kept secret when you enter this palapa-roof house with adobe walls a few blocks off the main strip. Sit on the front patio or in a backyard hut hung with weathered old lanterns and photographs of the Mexican Revolution. Menu highlights are *cabrilla con salsa de frambuesa* (sea bass with raspberry sauce), *camarón coco* (coconut shrimp with mango sauce), and the crab or fish with garlic sauce. A second menu, called Pasta Bella, offers a wide range of pastas and Italian dishes. *Guerrero and 5 de Mayo, tel. 624/105–1418. No credit cards. Closed Sun., no lunch.*

¢–$$ MAMA'S ROYAL CAFE/FELIX. Mama's serves up bountiful breakfasts of omelets, poached eggs with avocado and ham, and cream cheese-stuffed French toast topped with bananas and pecans. The fried potatoes are superb. At night, the colorful restaurant

Budget Bites

You can dine reasonably in Los Cabos if you're not scared by the myth that the food at mom-and-pop operations or at street stands will send you running for the bathroom. These places usually cook to order, so you can tell if something has been sitting out too long or hasn't been cooked well. If there's a crowd of locals, the food is probably fresh and well prepared. Safe bets include quesadillas, fish tacos, corn on the cob, and tortas (sandwiches). Some restaurants have a comida corrida (prepared lunch special), a three-course meal that consists of soup or salad, an entrée with rice and vegetables, coffee, and a small dessert. It's not gourmet, but you'll be sated economically.

In Cabo San Lucas, head for the taco stands behind Squid Roe and Avenida Cárdenas and the backstreets inland from the marina. **CARNITAS EL MICHOACANO** (Vicario between Carranza and Obregón) sells savory roasted pork served in tacos or tortas for about $3 each. At **POLLO DE ORO** (Morelos, at Av. Cárdenas, plus other locations), a half-chicken meal costs about $5. For inexpensive Mexican eateries close to the marina and hotels, try the juice stands. **RICO SUAVE** (Cardenas between Hidalgo and Guerrero) makes great smoothies with yogurt, as well as cheese tortas. **OYE COMO VA** (Guerrero and Zapata), a juice stand, also serves molletes (sliced rolls with beans and cheese) for $1.50.

CAFE EUROPA (Boulevard Marina) has a big breakfast burrito for $5 and quesadillas for $1.50. Listen for Beatles tunes playing night and day, and you'll find **GORDO'S TORTAS** (Guerrero and Zapata), where Gordo (named for his generous girth) sells ham and cheese tortas for about $2.

In San José del Cabo, there are at least a dozen stands at the **MERCADO MUNICIPAL.** You may be the only gringo at the tables—a great way to practice your Spanish. Stock up on fresh papayas, mangos, melons, and other peelable fruits. Look for reasonably priced restaurants on Zaragoza and Doblado by the market. Good taco stands line streets on the inland side of Highway 1. **SUPER TACOS INDIOS** has filling baked potatoes. **LAS RANAS,** a taquería (taco eatery), has a full bar.

shopping

LOS CABOS MANUFACTURES SUNSHINE AND A GOOD TIME but very few products. One exception is glassware from La Fábrica de Vidrio Soplado (Blown-Glass Factory). In addition, a burgeoning arts scene has national and international artists opening galleries. Several shops will custom-design gold and silver jewelry for you, fashioning pieces in one to two days. Liquor shops sell a locally produced liqueur called Damiana, touted as an aphrodisiac.

Despite Cabo's lack of homegrown wares, stores are filled with beautiful items from mainland Mexico. You can find hand-painted blue Talavera tiles from Puebla; blue-and-yellow pottery from Guanajuato; black pottery from the village of San Bartolo Coyotepec (near Oaxaca); hammocks from the Yucatán; embroidered clothing from Oaxaca, Chiapas, and the Yucatán; silver jewelry from Taxco; opals from Queretaro; and the fine beaded crafts of the Huichol tribe from Nayarit and Jalisco.

HOW & WHEN

Many stores, especially those that fan out from the central plaza in San José del Cabo and from the marina in San Lucas, open daily around 10 AM and close by 9 PM. Some shops still close at noon or 1 PM for a one- to two-hour lunch break. If cruise ships are in port, shops open early and stay open as long as the day-trippers are around.

Credit cards are widely accepted, though many places do not accept American Express. Most stores readily accept U.S. dollars

Bead by Bead

To place and glue the tiny beads that will turn a carved wooden jaguar the size of a small cat into a colorful work of art, it takes a Huichol Indian a full day—not to mention a steady hand. A small carving of a deer, considered a messenger of the gods to guide the shamans (priests who use magic to treat ailments) during ceremonies, may take only an hour. These unusual pieces can be found at the **HUICHOL COLLECTION** in Cabo San Lucas.

The sale of authentic ceremonial works of art, artifacts, and handicrafts helps to support the Huichol people. (The deer figurine, for instance, goes for about 200 pesos, or about $21.) Until recently, the Huichol, a tribe of shamans and artists, lived undisturbed in the rugged Sierra Madre in Nayarit and Jalisco. They are one of the few indigenous groups in the world to have retained their original culture. Approximately 8,000 still survive, keeping alive a spiritual, nature-based way of life.

but usually give change in pesos. Sticker prices appear in pesos or dollars—sometimes it's difficult to tell. Ask before you get too carried away, and carry a calculator for quick conversions.

Most enclosed shops do not bargain. Still, if you're buying a large quantity of items at one shop, you can always ask for a discount. Bargaining is acceptable when you go to a tianguis (arts-and-crafts market) and at the sidewalk market along the marina, but it may not be worth the effort.

Not all salespeople are fluent in English, especially in crafts shops, so use whatever Spanish you know and speak slowly.

NEIGHBORHOODS & MALLS
The palatial entrance to **PUERTO PARAÍSO** (Av. Cárdenas, Cabo San Lucas) leads into a three-story marble and glass-enclosed

mall. Though at this writing, the mall is not yet full, it's quickly becoming a social center of San Lucas. Kaki Bassi, a well-known local artist, has opened a gallery, as has Sergio Bustamante. Clothing shops include Cotton Club, Guess, and quicksilver, plus several beachwear boutiques. If you're hungry, check out the two Häagen-Dazs shops, Johnny Rockets diner, or Ruth's Chris Steak House. A bowling alley and a complex of movie theaters take care of your entertainment needs.

PLAZA ARAMBURO (Av. Cárdenas and Av. Zaragoza, Cabo San Lucas) is a primarily service-oriented shopping area with a pharmacy, bank, dry cleaner, and grocery store. But it also has clothing and swimwear shops. A pleasant place to stroll, **PLAZA BONITA** (Blvd. Marina at Av. Cárdenas, Cabo San Lucas) has restaurants, bars, and a few shops. **PLAZA DEL MAR** (Av. Cárdenas, Cabo San Lucas), across from the Plaza Bonita mall, sells T-shirts, tank tops, sweatshirts, and more at its souvenir boutiques. Bordering the Cabo San Lucas marina is the **PLAZA NAUTICA** (Blvd. Marina, Cabo San Lucas), where you can find resort wear, jewelry, furniture, fine art, and a number of eateries. Near where the fishing boats come in at the Cabo San Lucas marina, the **MERCADO DE ARTESANÍAS** (Crafts Market; south end of Blvd. Marina, Cabo San Lucas) sells pottery, blankets, jewelry, and Mexican sombreros.

SPECIALTY SHOPS

Cabo San Lucas

The aroma of roasting coffee beans lures caffeine junkies to ★**THE CABO COFFEE COMPANY** (Madero at Hidalgo, tel. 624/105–1130). The store sells flavored coffee, chai tea, and ice cream as well.

★ **EL CALLEJÓN** (Guerrero between Av. Cárdenas and Madero, tel. 624/143–1139) is known for gorgeous furniture, lamps, dishes, and pottery. **CARTES** (Plaza Bonita, Blvd. Marina, tel. 624/143–

People in Glass Houses

A beautiful glass mosaic over the entrance to La Fábrica de Vidrio Soplado (Blown-Glass Factory) welcomes Los Cabos's most famous artisans every day. Founded in 1988 by engineer Sebastian Romo, the factory uses a glassmaking process close to the one first developed in western Asia 4,000 years ago, later refined into glassblowing during the Roman empire.

At the factory, 35 artisans produce more than 450 pieces a day from hundreds of pounds of locally recycled glass. Tourists watch while crushed recycled glass is liquefied in gas-fired ovens and, seconds later, transformed into exquisite figures. Secrets for making the thick glassware's deep blues, greens, and reds— the result of special mixtures of metals and gold—are passed from generation to generation.

You are sometimes invited to make your own glassware by blowing through a hollow rod to shape a glob of molten glass at the end. The results are usually not impressive. The factory is in the industrial area of Cabo San Lucas and is usually open to the public Monday through Saturday 8 AM to 2 PM.

1770) has hand-painted pottery and tableware, pewter frames, handblown glass, and carved furniture.

Choose from the many serapes and cotton blankets at **CUCA'S BLANKET FACTORY** (Av. Cárdenas at Matamoros, tel. 624/143–1913). You can design your own and have it ready the next day. **DOS LUNAS** (Plaza Bonita, Blvd. Marina, tel. 624/143–1969) has a trendy selection of colorful sportswear. Handblown glass pieces in vivid colors are sold at **LA FÁBRICA DE VIDRIO SOPLADO** (Blown-Glass Factory; 2 blocks west of Hwy. 1, tel. 624/143–0255) on the outskirts of Cabo San Lucas. Drive toward San José on Avenida Cárdenas, which turns into Highway 1. The factory is in an industrial area two blocks northwest of Highway 1, off the bypass to Todos Santos.

One of the oldest folk art shops in the area, **FACES OF MEXICO** (Av. Cárdenas, beside the Mar de Cortés hotel, tel. 624/143–2634) has a selection of masks from Oaxaca and Guerrero, though the owner's collection of handmade masks at the back of the tiny shop is far more interesting than the manufactured versions for sale up front.

Walk around the marina from Plaza Bonita to **GALERIA GATEMELATTA** (Calle Gómez Farias, the road to the Hotel Hacienda, tel. 624/143–1166), where the specialties are colonial furniture and antiques. The second-floor ★**GOLDEN CACTUS GALLERY** (Guerrero and Madero, tel. 624/143–6399), run by artists Chris MacClure and Marilyn Hurst, has been showcasing local artists' work since 1997. Bill Clinton is among those with MacClure's pieces in their collections.

At **HARLEY DAVIDSON** (Puerto Paraíso, Av. Cárdenas, tel. 624/143–3337), you can rent a Harley for about $200 a day. The **HUICHOL COLLECTION** (Blvd. Marina and Ocampo, tel. 624/143–4055) carries the Huichol Indian tribe's beautiful beaded crafts, as well as posters, postcards, and T-shirts in the vibrant colors and patterns typical of this ancient culture.

Cuban and international cigars are sold at **J&J HABANOS** (Madero and Blvd. Marina, tel. 624/143–6160), as is tequila, Cuban coffee, and clothing. Gorgeous silver jewelry created by the Brilanti family of Taxco is on display at ★**JOYERÍA BRILANTI** (Guerrero between Madero and Zapata, tel. 624/105–1664, www.brilanti.com). The family's work has been included in museum shows in the United States and is coveted by collectors.

The ★**KAKI BASSI GALLERY** (Morelos and Alikan, tel. 624/143–3510; Puerto Paraíso, Av. Cárdenas, tel. 624/144–4510) displays works by Kaki Bassi, who has exhibited all over Europe and has seven pieces of art in the Mexican government's permanent collection. Her gallery exhibits many Mexican artists. **LIBROS** (Blvd. Marina at Plaza de la Danza, tel. 624/143–3173) carries a vast number of Spanish- and English-language novels and magazines.

A favorite of locals and Cabo regulars, ★**MAGIC OF THE MOON** (Hidalgo off Blvd. Marina, tel. 624/143–3161) has unique clothing designed by Pepita, the owner. If you don't see what you want, she can design an outfit for you and have it made in three days. Check out her handmade ceramic jewelry and beaded bustiers. **MAMA ELI'S** (Av. San Lucas, tel. 624/143–1616) is a three-story gallery with fine furnishings, ceramics, appliquéd clothing, and children's toys. **NECRI** (Blvd. Marina between Madero and Ocampo, tel. 624/143–0283) has an excellent selection of folk art and home furnishings.

Locals appreciate the selection of imported wines, cheeses, pâtés, and other gourmet delicacies, including organic foods, at **TUTTO BENE** (Blvd. Marina near Calle San Lucas, tel. 624/144–3300).

San José del Cabo

San José has the best shopping for high-quality folk art, jewelry, and home furnishings. Some of the finest shops are clustered around Plaza Mijares where Boulevard Mijares and Avenida Zaragoza both end at a pedestrian walkway.

AMETHYST (Blvd. Mijares and Doblado, tel. 624/142–4160) carries rings, bracelets, and necklaces with precious and semiprecious stones, including Mexican opal. Custom designs can be made in a few hours; complex designs may take a couple of days. **COPAL** (Plaza Mijares, tel. 624/142–3070) has a nice selection of carved animals from Oaxaca and hammocks from the Yucatán. **CURIOS ALBERTO** (Av. Zaragoza in front of Plaza Mijares, no phone) carries beautiful embroidered dresses for young girls.

★ **GALERÍA VERYKA** (Blvd. Mijares 6-B, tel. 624/142–0575) is the best folk art shop in the region, with gorgeous embroidered clothing, masks, wood carvings, jewelry, and hand-molded black and green pottery. Nearly everything is from Oaxaca. **SAX** (Blvd. Mijares 2, tel. 624/142–6053) displays handcrafted silver jewelry. The artists will create a design of your choice in 24 hours.

LOS BARRILES DE CUERVO (Blvd. Mijares at Juárez, tel. 624/142–5322) specializes in rare tequilas. The bookstore **LIBROS** (Blvd. Mijares 41, tel. 624/142–4433) stocks a good selection of magazines, as well as the *Wall Street Journal* and *USA Today*.

Several gems are clustered along the side streets off Mijares. **ARTE, DISEÑO Y DECORACIÓN** (ADD; Av. Zaragoza at Calle Hidalgo, tel. 624/143–2055) is an interior-design shop that has hand-painted dishes from Guanajuato, carved wood furniture from Michoacán, and unique Christmas decorations. **AMIGOS SMOKESHOP & CIGAR BAR** (Calle Doblado and Morelos, tel. 624/142–1138) is a classy shop and cigar bar with fine Cuban and Mexican cigars and Casa Noble tequila. Look for visiting celebrities here. Away from the tourist zone is San José's traditional market area, **EL MERCADO SAN JOSÉ** (Castro at Coronado, no phone), where you can stock your kitchen(ette) with fresh meats and produce.

The Corridor

Along the Corridor, shopping is limited to hotel gift shops, a couple of artisans' markets that cater to busloads of cruise-ship passengers, a few strip malls, and a Costco warehouse store. The shop at the **HOTEL CABO SAN LUCAS** (Hwy. 1, Km 14.5, tel. 624/144–0014) has one of the best collections of jewelry, pottery, and crafts in the Corridor. **LA EUROPA** (Hwy. 1, Km 6.7, tel. 624/145–8755) carries a wide selection of imported wines and deli products. **TRADER DICK'S** (Hwy. 1, Km 29.5, tel. 624/142–2828) is a favorite with Americans seeking newspapers from home, along with familiar deli meats and cheeses.

For nearly three hours, the man struggles to reel it in. Finally, the flailing marlin breaks the water's surface, soaking him to the bone. Amid surges of pain and exhilaration, the Old Man and the Sea flashes through his wearying head. He uses what's left of his wit and strength, and his reward is there, thrashing about aboard the skiff. The 400-pound beauty soon will be released back into the sea, but the snapshots will be proof enough.

In This Chapter

By Brad Weiss

Revised by Maribeth Mellin

beaches &
water sports

LONG STRETCHES OF COASTLINE along the Sea of Cortez and the Pacific Ocean allow for plenty of fun in the sand and surf. Add to that nearly 360 warm and sunny days per year, and you get a natural wonderland where outdoor activities can be enjoyed year-round. During winter, tourists from the north flock to this sun-licked playground to soak up the rays and challenge the waves. In the summer, tourists and locals alike head to the water for a break from the intense heat.

From crowded people-watching beaches to secluded coves, high-speed Jet Ski rides to leisurely fishing trips, and daring deep-sea scuba expeditions to casual snorkeling, the waters off Cabo offer endless possibilities.

HOW & WHEN

Most beaches in the area stay mob-free. The exception is Playa Médano, which is alongside Cabo San Lucas. Most people on this beach, however, are searching for crowds. None of the other beaches are within walking distance of either Cabo San Lucas or San José del Cabo; some can be accessed by boat, but most require a car ride (unless you are staying at a Corridor hotel nearby). You can reach nearly all the beaches by bus, but it may take a while. None of the beaches charges an admission fee.

BEACHES

Beneath the rocky cliffs of the Pacific Ocean and the Sea of Cortez lie many bays, coves, and unprotected swaths of sandy beach. The waters range from translucent green to deep navy, from calm to turbulent. Playa Médano, in Cabo San Lucas, is the most visited and active stretch of sand. Gorgeous and somewhat secluded Playa del Amor (Lover's Beach) is five minutes across the bay by water taxi. Just southwest of San José, the most popular beaches are Costa Azul and Playa Palmilla.

Bahía Santa María and Bahía Chileno are two beautiful strands in the Corridor. But for some truly secluded gems, drive an hour or two north of either town. Perhaps the most stunning and desolate beaches in the area are in Cabo Pulmo, 1½ hours north of San José or 2 hours from Cabo San Lucas.

★ **BAHÍA CHILENO.** Ideal for swimming and snorkeling, this pretty Corridor beach skirts a small, crescent-shape cove with aquamarine water. On the western end stands a rocky cliff where the Hotel Cabo San Lucas is perched. Along the eastern edge, some 200 yards away, are boulders you can climb. On the trek down you may see some stray wrappers and cans, but the beach itself is clean and usually not too crowded. During winter, this part of the Sea of Cortez gets chilly—refreshing for a dip, but most snorkelers cut their swims short.

The only business on the beach is **Cabo Acuadeportes** (tel. 624/ 143–0117), which rents snorkel equipment and offers scuba diving and snorkeling trips to nearby sites; hours are erratic. The turnoff for the beach is near the Hotel Cabo San Lucas, Km 14.5 on the Transpeninsular Highway (Hwy. 1). There is a sign; from San José turn immediately after the hotel; from San Lucas, just before. *16 km (9 mi) west of San José del Cabo, 16 km (9 mi) east of Cabo San Lucas.*

★ **BAHÍA SANTA MARÍA.** Rugged brown cliffs protect this picture-perfect tan-sand cove. Though as uncrowded as Bahía Chileno, this bay is better for snorkeling: hundreds of brightly colored fish swarm through chunks of white coral. No shop is set up, but there is usually someone on the beach renting snorkeling gear for $10 per day. From San José del Cabo, take a left off Highway 1 about 2½ km (1¼ mi) after the Hotel Cabo San Lucas; from San Lucas, watch for a sign on the right of Highway 1 designating the beach turnoff. Take your second left at the sign that reads ACCESO A ZONA FEDERAL (access to federal zone). *19 km (11 mi) west of San José del Cabo, 13 km (8 mi) east of Cabo San Lucas.*

PLAYA DEL AMOR. The most-photographed beach in Cabo is in a secluded cove at the very end of the Baja peninsula, where the Sea of Cortez meets the Pacific Ocean. The contrast between the peaceful azure cove on the Sea of Cortez and the pounding white Pacific surf is dramatic. El Arco (the Arch), a natural rock archway, towers over the white sand. Craggy rock formations form small caves. You can explore them, but you might find little more than trash and foul smells.

Swimming and snorkeling are best on the Sea of Cortez, where the clear green, almost luminescent water is unquestionably the nicest in San Lucas. The Pacific side is too turbulent for swimming but ideal for relatively secluded sunbathing. Vendors are scarce, so bring your own snacks and plenty of water. The beach is crowded at times, but never like Playa Médano. To get here, take a five-minute water-taxi ride or a 15- to 20-minute glass-bottom boat tour. Opt for the latter if you want to photograph the Arch from the Pacific. Both leave from the Cabo San Lucas marina or Playa Médano every hour until 3 PM. Contact **Pisces Water Sports** (Playa Médano, tel. 044–624/148–7530 cell phone) for information about the glass-bottom boat tour. *Just outside Cabo San Lucas, at El Arco.*

PLAYA CERRITOS. This long, expansive beach on the Pacific Ocean is famous among surfers for breaking wonderful waves during winter. Even if you don't ride the waves, you can watch them crash along the shore. The vast, unspoiled beauty of this

Surf's Up

The tip of Baja is rife with surfing spots—no secret to the hordes of wave riders who swarm here year-round. Right breaks dominate, but left breaks can be found at La Bocana (just outside San José del Cabo) and Playa Monumentos (the Corridor, near Misiones del Cabo Hotel).

At La Bocana, a freshwater estuary, giant tubes are created when heavy rains open the river mouth. Monumentos has consistently gut-wrenching waves. Little-known Nueve Palmas (Nine Palms), halfway between San José del Cabo and Cabo Pulmo, has a right break perfect for long-boarders.

In summer, Costa Azul is the beach of choice; its world-famous, experts-only Zippers break often tops 12 feet. Next-best is Shipwrecks on the East Cape, about a half hour north of San José by car. In winter, surfers in the know head to the Pacific side to Los Cerritos, near Todos Santos. The large waves and expansive, rockless beach are ideal. Wherever you go, be respectful of local surfers, who know these waters well.

soft-sand beach make a visit worthwhile. Swimming is not recommended because of the strong currents.

Most of the surfing crowd camps or stays in RVs near the beach. The fairly secluded area covers the basics with a few conveniences—including water, a small food stand, and a surf shop. The beach is 2½ km (1½ mi) from Highway 19, which connects Cabo San Lucas and Todos Santos. 65 km (40 mi) north of Cabo San Lucas, 13 km (8 mi) south of Todos Santos.

PLAYA COSTA AZUL. Cabo's best surfing beach is especially popular in summer, when the waves are largest. Costa Azul's Zippers "break" (the point where the wave crests and breaks) is world-famous. Other highly regarded breaks are La Roca (the Rock) and the made-for-beginners Old Man's break. The strong undercurrent makes swimming too dangerous here.

Extending 3 km (2 mi) south from San José's hotel zone, Costa Azul also encompasses the beaches closer to town that are sometimes referred to as Playa California and Playa Hotelera. Condo complexes and hotels line much of the beach; restaurants are a block or two inland. *Just southwest of San José.*

☝ **PLAYA MÉDANO.** Less than 2 km (1 mi) from the town center, this beach is the most popular daytime destination in Cabo San Lucas. It is not especially attractive, but the water is calm enough for swimming. Pollution can be a concern, however, especially after strong rains, when the preponderance of motorized boats and water toys leaves a bit of an oil slick. The shore hosts plenty of distractions: bar-restaurants, hotels, water sports, volleyball nets, and boat tours.

The 3-km (2-mi) span of beach begins at the marina and extends well past the main hotel cluster. The most popular area is around several bar-restaurants, where beach chairs and tables are set up. This is a hot spot for people-watching (and for singles seeking to be doubles). Be prepared to deal with the many crafts vendors cruising the beach. They're generally not pushy, so a simple head shake will do. *Paseo del Pescador, Cabo San Lucas.*

PLAYA PALMILLA. The best swimming beach near San José del Cabo is protected by a rocky point just south of town. Fleets of pangas (small skiffs) are clustered on the sand, but there's plenty of space for sunbathing and swimming in calm water. *Entrance on Hwy. 1, at Km 27, 8 km (5 mi) southwest of San José del Cabo, the Corridor.*

PLAYA SOLMAR. This long, uncrowded Pacific Ocean beach is divorced from Playa del Amor by a large rock formation. You can hike from here to Playa del Amor during low tide, but keep an eye on the water to gauge your return. The beautiful, often deserted beach has such a powerful undertow that swimming is extremely dangerous. Four resorts—Solmar, Terrasol, Playa Grande, and Finisterra—are all on this beach, but guests tend to stick to the hotel pools. *Blvd. Marina to the hotel entrances, Cabo San Lucas.*

PLAYA LAS VIUDAS (TWIN DOLPHIN BEACH). Beneath the Twin Dolphin Hotel, this small public beach is great for snorkeling (bring your own gear). Low tides reveal great tidal pools filled with anemone, starfish, and other sea creatures. Take the access road directly south of the hotel. *Hwy. 1, Km 12, the Corridor.*

WATER SPORTS

Waterskiing, jet skiing, parasailing, and sailing are found almost exclusively at Playa Médano, where you can also go kayaking and boating. At least eight good scuba-diving sites are near Playa del Amor. Cabo Pulmo, which has the only coral reef in the Sea of Cortez, has even more. Snorkeling is also popular. Both the Sea of Cortez and the Pacific ensure great waves for year-round surfing. Still, in this uncontested "Marlin Capital of the World," sportfishing is perhaps the most famous water sport.

Fishing

There are more than 800 species of fish in the waters off Los Cabos, and some anglers seem determined to catch them all. The most popular quarry are the huge blue, black, and striped marlin, which leap with glistening majesty in the sea. Anglers more interested in putting the catch-of-the-day on the table aim for dorado (called mahimahi in Hawaii), tuna, and wahoo. Something's always biting, but the greatest diversity of species swim Cabo waters from June to November.

Fishing charters arranged through hotels or sportfishing companies include a captain and crew, tackle, bait, licenses, drinks, and sometimes lunch. Prices start at $325 per half-day for a 28-foot cruiser that can carry two or three passengers. A larger cruiser with a head (bathroom) and sunbathing space

Fishing for Dollars

The busiest time in Los Cabos is neither Christmas nor Spring Break but rather the last week of October—when the world's most prestigious marlin fishing tournament, the **BISBEE BLACK & BLUE JACKPOT MARLIN TOURNAMENT,** takes place. More than 200 boat crews come from around the world in attempts to claim prizes totaling more than $1 million. Boats range from 28-foot skiffs to 100-foot (and larger) yachts. The only qualification necessary is the entry fee, which is more than $15,000.

Prizes are awarded to those who haul in the greatest size and quantity of blue and black marlins during the three-day tournament. In 2003, the prize for a 565-pound blue marlin was a record-breaking $1,165,230. Marlins under 500 pounds aren't even counted; the largest single catch ever weighed in at 1,080 pounds. Even with state-of-the-art equipment and perfect techniques, each marlin takes at least two hours to reel in. The especially large and feisty ones have had crews struggling for up to eight hours. Once caught, the marlins are either released or donated to onlookers at the dock.

starts at about $400—from here, the sky's the limit. Private boats have air-conditioned staterooms, hot-water showers, full kitchens, and every other imaginable amenity. Pangas (small motorized skiffs) with a skipper rent for about $180–$200 for six hours. They're most comfortable with one or two passengers. Companies typically try to help solo anglers hook up with a group to share a boat.

Vendors along the harbor-front offer all sorts of fishing options. To choose the best one for you, hang out at the harbor between 1 PM and 4 PM when the boats come in and ask the passengers about their experiences.

Anglers are strongly encouraged to release any fish they won't eat, rather than bring them in as trophies. Marlin are often hauled in to be weighed for photos and then discarded because the meat is not very tasty. The fish you bring in can be weighed and filleted at the docks, and vendors are available to take your catch away to be frozen, smoked, or canned. Most restaurants gladly prepare your catch any way you like. Nearly all boats leave from the Cabo San Lucas harbor, either from the sportfishing docks at the south end of the harbor or from behind the Plaza Las Glorias Hotel.

At the long-established **SOLMAR FLEET** (Blvd. Marina, Cabo San Lucas, across from the sportfishing dock, tel. 624/143–0646, 624/143–4542, or 800/344–3349, www.solmar.com), boats and tackle are always in good shape, and regulars wouldn't fish with anyone else. The **GAVIOTA FLEET** (Bahía Condo hotel, Playa Médano, Cabo San Lucas, tel. 624/143–0430 or 800/932–5599, www.grupobahia.com) currently holds the record for the largest marlin caught in Cabo's waters. The company has charter cruisers and pangas. Some of the Corridor's priciest hotels choose the **PISCES SPORTFISHING FLEET** (Cabo Maritime Center, Blvd. Marina, Cabo San Lucas, tel. 624/143–1288, www.piscessportfishing.com). The fleet includes the usual 31-foot Bertrams, plus 50- to 70-foot Hatteras cruisers with tuna towers and staterooms.

For a private boat that carries six or more passengers, contact **CORTEZ YACHT CHARTERS** (3609 Hartzel Dr., Spring Valley, CA 91977, tel. 619/469–4299 in the U.S., www.cortezcharters.com). **VICTOR'S SPORT FISHING** (Playa Palmilla, the Corridor, tel. 624/142–1092) has long been a favorite for its pangas with shade awnings and plastic seats. The outfitter also has cruisers. The boats at **GORDO BANKS PANGAS** (La Playa, near San José del Cabo, tel. 624/142–1147, 800/408–1199 in the U.S., www.gordobanks.com) push off from shore near some of the hottest fishing spots in the Sea of Cortez—the famed outer and inner Gordo Banks. Renowned tackle store **MINERVA'S** (Madero, between Blvd. Marina and Guerrero, Cabo San Lucas, tel. 624/143–1282, www.minervas.com) has four charter-fishing boats. Fishing gear and line are available at **DEPORTIVA PISCIS FISHING TACKLE SHOP** (Calle Mauricio Castro, San José del Cabo, near the Mercado Municipal, tel. 624/142–0332). **JIG STOP TOURS** (34186 Coast Hwy., Dana Point, CA 92629, tel. 800/521–2281 in the U.S., www.jigstop.com) books fishing trips for several Los Cabos fleets.

Jet Skiing & Waterskiing

Several operators offer comparable, if not identical, prices. Both jet skiing and waterskiing cost about $45 for a half hour and $70 for a full hour.

JT WATER SPORTS (Playa Médano, Cabo San Lucas, tel. 624/144–4566) has every type of water- and land-sports equipment, including diving gear, waverunners, Windsurfers, and parasails. Waverunners rent for $80 an hour; parasailing costs $40. **OMEGA SPORTS** (three locations on Playa Médano, Cabo San Lucas, tel. 624/143–5519) offers jet skiing. **PISCES WATERSPORTS** (far side of Playa Médano, Cabo San Lucas, tel. 044–624/148–7530 cell phone) is a large operation with jet skiing and waterskiing. It also rents Hobie Cats by the hour, gives 12-minute rides on banana boats (long, yellow inflatable rafts towed by high-speed motorboats), and rents water-sports equipment. **TIO SPORTS** (Playa Médano, Cabo San Lucas, by Meliá San Lucas, tel. 624/143–3399) is a large operator with stands and offices throughout Los Cabos.

Kayaking

The most popular and practical way to explore the pristine coves that dot the Los Cabos shoreline is by kayak. Daylong package tours that combine kayaking with snorkeling or scuba diving cost anywhere from $60 to $125. Single or double kayaks can be rented by the hour for $10 to $20.

CABO PULMO

In addition to the awesome beauty of the water, close-range views of a sea-lion colony attract kayakers to Cabo Pulmo. For a combined kayak and snorkeling trip, try **BAJA SALVAJE** (Obregón at Guerrero, San José del Cabo, tel. 624/148–2222 or 624/142–5300, www.bajawild.com), also called Wild Baja. Daylong trips include transportation, equipment, and lunch; you may substitute scuba diving for snorkeling. A full-day tour costs $95. If you have your own transportation to Cabo Pulmo, you can rent a kayak or take a trip with **CABO PULMO BEACH RESORT** (Hwy. 1 at La Ribera turnoff, tel. 624/141–0244, www.cabopulmo.com). A six-hour guided tour to the sea-lion colony and environs includes lunch and snorkeling gear; tours depart at 9 AM.

PLAYA MÉDANO

OMEGA SPORTS (Playa Médano, tel. 624/143–5519) has good rates on single and double kayaks. **CABO ACUADEPORTES** (Hotel Hacienda, Playa Médano, tel. 624/143–0117, www.cabowatersports.com) has snorkeling and waterskiing, as well as good prices on kayak rentals. **TIO SPORTS** (Playa Médano, tel. 624/143–3399, www.tiosports.com) has kayak rentals and packages that include snorkeling. **JT WATER SPORTS** (Playa Médano, tel. 624/144–4566) rents kayaks on the beach.

SAN JOSÉ DEL CABO

Kayak tours and rentals are available through **LOS LOBOS DEL MAR** (Brisas del Mar RV park, on the south side of San José, tel. 624/142–2983). The tours paddle along the Corridor's peaceful bays and are especially fun in winter when gray whales pass by offshore. Rates start at $30.

Parasailing & Sailing

Parasailing costs between $30 and $40 for an eight-minute flight. Most operators won't tell you the stories about broken

An Underwater Paradise

One of Baja's true gems is Cabo Pulmo, the raw, unspoiled national marine preserve along the Sea of Cortez. More than 5 mi of nearly deserted rocky beach border the only living coral-reef system on the Sea of Cortez. Several dive sites reveal hundreds of species of tropical fish, large schools of manta rays, and a sea-lion colony. This is a nearly perfect place for scuba diving and snorkeling.

The village of Cabo Pulmo has 100 or so residents, depending on the season. Power comes from solar panels, and drinking water is trucked in over dirt roads. Near the beach, solar-powered cottages are for rent at the **CABO PULMO BEACH RESORT** (Cabo Pulmo, tel. 624/141–0244, www.cabopulmo.com), which also has a full-service PADI dive facility. The town has two small general stores and three restaurants. Cabo Pulmo is a magnet for serious divers, kayakers, and windsurfers and remains one of southern Baja's natural treasures.

ropes, so proceed at your own risk. Sailboats and Windsurfers average about $20 per hour.

CABO ACUADEPORTES (Hotel Hacienda, Playa Médano, Cabo San Lucas, tel. 624/143–0117; Bahía Chileno, 16 km (9 mi) west of San José del Cabo, 16 km (9 mi) east of Cabo San Lucas), one of the oldest operators in the area, rents Windsurfers and Sunfish sailboats. Both can be rented by the hour. This is the first shop on Playa Médano when coming from the Cabo San Lucas marina. Parasails are among the many types of water-sports gear available at **JT WATER SPORTS** (Playa Médano, Cabo San Lucas, tel. 624/144–4566).

Scuba Diving

One of the pioneers of diving in the area was none other than Jacques Cousteau, who explored the **SAND FALLS.** Only 150 feet off Playa del Amor, this underwater sand river cascades off a steep drop-off into a deep abyss. In fact, this is one of several excellent diving or snorkeling spots close to the Cabo San Lucas shore. There are also fantastic coral-reef sites in the Corridor and north of San José.

OPERATORS

All operators offer essentially the same dives, at comparable prices. Generally, diving costs about $45 for one tank and $70 for two, including transportation. Equipment rental, dives in the Corridor, and night dives typically cost extra. Full-day trips to Gordo Banks and Cabo Pulmo cost about $125, including transportation, food, equipment, and two tanks. Most operators offer two- to four-day package deals.

Most dive shops have courses for noncertified divers; some may be offered through your hotel. Newly certified divers may go on local dives no more than 20 feet deep. Divers must show their C-card (diver certification card) before going on dives with reputable shops. Many operators offer widely recognized Professional Association of Diving Instructors (PADI) certification courses.

AMIGOS DEL MAR (Blvd. Marina, Cabo San Lucas, near harbor fishing docks, tel. 624/143–0505, 800/344-3349 in the U.S., www.amigosdelmar.com) is the oldest and most complete dive shop in the Los Cabos area. The staff is courteous and knowledgeable, and all guides speak English. **CABO ACUADEPORTES** (Hotel Hacienda, Playa Médano, Cabo San Lucas, tel. 624/143–0117; Bahía Chileno, 16 km (9 mi) west of San José del Cabo, 16 km (9 mi) east of Cabo San Lucas) has boat dives from its shop on Playa Médano and boat and shore dives from its shop at Chileno Bay in the Corridor. The **SOLMAR V** (Solmar Suites hotel, Blvd. Marina, Cabo San Lucas, tel. 624/143–0022, 800/344-3349 in the U.S., www.solmar.com), a luxury dive boat, takes weeklong trips to the islands of

Socorro, San Benedicto, and Clarion, as well as to the coral reefs at Cabo Pulmo. Twelve cabins with private baths serve a maximum of 24 passengers.

WHERE TO DIVE

At all of the sites in **BAHÍA SAN LUCAS** near El Arco you're likely to see colorful tropical fish traveling confidently in large schools. Yellow angelfish, green and blue parrotfish, red snappers, perfectly camouflaged stonefish, and long, slender needlefish share these waters. Divers regularly encounter stingrays, manta rays, and moray eels. The only problem with this location is the amount of boat traffic. The sound of motors penetrates deep into the water and can slightly mar the experience. The **SEA-LION COLONY** at Cabo Pulmo makes for a fun dive most of the year—except in summer, when these residents swim back out to sea. **NEPTUNE'S FINGERS** (60–120 feet) is a long rock formation with abundant fish. About 150 feet off Playa del Amor, **PELICAN ROCK** (25–100 feet) is a calm, protected spot where you can look down on Sand Falls. **THE POINT** (15–80 feet) is a good spot for beginners who aren't ready to get too deep.

The Corridor has four popular diving sites. **BAHÍA SANTA MARIA** (20–60 feet) has water clear enough to see hard and soft corals, octopus, eels, and many tropical fish. **CHILENO REEF** (10–80 feet) is a protected finger reef 1 km (½ mi) from Chileno Bay, with many invertebrates, including starfish, flower urchins, and hydroids. The **BLOW-HOLE** (60–100 feet) is known for diverse terrain—massive boulders, rugged tunnels, shallow caverns, and deep rock cuts—which house manta rays, sea turtles, and large schools of amberjacks and grouper. The **SHIPWRECK** (40–60 feet), an old Japanese fishing boat, is close to Cabo San Lucas, near the Misiones del Cabo hotel.

Three very unique diving spots can be found beyond the local area. The best spot for tropical fish and rays in the greater Los Cabos area is in the coral-reef system of the marine preserve at **CABO PULMO** (15–130 feet). The water is so clear that visibility can exceed 100 feet in summer. Expert divers head to **GORDO BANKS** (100–130 feet), also known as the Wahoo Banks, which are 13 km (8 mi) off the coast of San José. The currents are too strong for less experienced divers. This is the spot for hammerhead sharks—not generally aggressive with divers—many species of tropical fish and rays, and, if you're lucky, dolphins. Fall is the best time to go. Well off the coast of **LA PAZ** (15–130 feet) you may find hammerhead and whale sharks.

Snorkeling

Many of the best dive spots are also good for snorkeling. Prime areas include the waters surrounding **PLAYA DEL AMOR, BAHÍA SANTA MARÍA, BAHÍA CHILENO,** and **CABO PULMO.** Nearly all scuba operators also offer snorkel rentals and trips. Equipment rentals generally cost $10 per hour. Two-hour guided trips to Playa del Amor are about $25; day trips to Cabo Pulmo cost about $60.

BOAT TOURS

The most upscale boat in the Los Cabos area is a beautiful 48-foot catamaran called **LA PRINCESA** (Cabo San Lucas Harbor, Cabo San Lucas, tel. 624/143–7676). Daily trips to Bahía Santa María or Bahía Chileno depart between noon and 3 PM. For $49 per person, you get drinks, a light lunch, and equipment. **OCEANUS** (Blvd. Marina, Cabo San Lucas, by El Galeon restaurant, tel. 624/143–3929) leaves at 11 AM for snorkeling cruises. **PEZ GATO** (Plaza Las Glorias, Cabo San Lucas, tel. 624/143–3797) has several cruising options including a $39-per-person snorkeling trip. **JUNGLE CRUISE** (Plaza Las Glorias, Cabo San Lucas, tel. 624/143–8150) has slightly smaller, less-luxurious boats that draw a young, party-oriented crowd. Four-hour trips cost $35 and include drinks, a light lunch, and equipment. **BUCCANEER QUEEN** (Solmar Hotel, Cabo San Lucas, tel. 624/144–4217) is a tall ship used in TV commercials that now carries passengers on snorkeling and sunset cruises.

Surfing

BAJA SALVAJE (Obregón at Guerrero, San José del Cabo, tel. 624/
148–2222 or 624/142–5300, www.bajawild.com) has daylong
trips to surfing hot spots for beginners and experts. A fee of $65
per person includes transportation, equipment, and instruction
at Costa Azul. Surf tours on the Pacific cost $85 per person. For
good surfing tips, rentals, and lessons, head to **COSTA AZUL
SURF SHOP** (Hwy. 1, Km 27.5, the Corridor, tel. 624/142–2771,
www.costa-azul.com.mx). Surfboard rentals are $20 a day and
lessons are $25 an hour. You can rent a board right on the beach
at **TODOS SANTOS SURF SHOP** (Playa Los Cerritos, Hwy. 19, Km
64, near Todos Santos, tel. 044–612/108–0709 cell phone).

From a distance, the 17th hole seems to teeter on the edge of a rocky precipice. He harbors fleeting thoughts of diving into the crashing waves below. But drawing closer, he realizes that the jagged slope gives way to an immaculate green fairway flanked by cactus fields. His gaze moves over the oasislike green amid a beach greeting the Sea of Cortez. "Play or stray? That is the question," he thinks impulsively.

In This Chapter

Revised by Maribeth Mellin

other outdoor
activities & sports

IN THIS OCEAN-SIDE PLAYGROUND, where sportfishing reigns supreme, the sea has long been the center for most activities. But Cabo's terrain lends itself to many sports and activities as well. Cactus fields, sand dunes, waterfalls, and mountain forests can be explored on foot, horseback, and on ATVs (all-terrain vehicles). Several tall rock faces make the area ideal for climbing and rappelling. Back in town, you can play beach volleyball on Playa Médano, tennis at most hotels or at the Fonatur complex, and get in a workout at your hotel or one of several gyms. For a less physically demanding outdoor activity, you can take a whale-watching or sunset cruise on one of the many tour boats.

Golf has lately become one of the biggest draws in Los Cabos. Much of the area's resources are being invested in the development of championship golf courses that serve as the centerpieces for enormous tourism developments.

AIR TOURS

One of the most spectacular ways to view Baja is from the air. **AÉREO CALAFIA** (Blvd. Marina at Plaza las Glorias, Cabo San Lucas, tel. 624/143–4302, www.aereocalafia.com) offers flights in small planes to Magdalena Bay where gray whales cave during winter months. The tours include the flight, a boat tour among the whales, and lunch, for $385 per person. Aéreo Calafia also offers air charters and specialized tours.

ATV TOURS

This is one of the most thrilling yet dangerous activities in Los Cabos. According to the local ambulance company, two or three people are injured every day (mostly sprains and broken bones). Accidents usually occur when operators take out huge groups with too few guides, lead them through major thoroughfares, and offer little or no instruction or safety tips. Know your trip's itinerary ahead of time. None of the companies have insurance, and they make you sign away your rights before going. But they do issue helmets, goggles, and handkerchiefs to protect you from the sand and dust.

When ATV trips are properly conducted, they can be safe and fun. The most popular trip passes through desert cactus fields, arrives at a big play area of large sand dunes with open expanses and specially carved trails, and ends at the old lighthouse. You can reach frighteningly high speeds as you descend the tall dunes. Navigating the narrow trails in the cactus fields is exciting but not for the weak-hearted or steering-impaired; you need to make sharp turns to avoid scraping into cactus, getting stuck in the sand, or toppling over. Another favorite trek travels past interesting rock formations, little creeks, and the beach on its way to a small mountain village called La Candelaria.

A three-hour trip costs about $50 for a single or $70 for a double (two people sharing an ATV). Six-hour trips to La Candelaria include lunch and cost about $90 for a single and $110 for a double. Wear tennis shoes, clothes you don't mind getting dirty, and a long-sleeve shirt or sweatshirt for afternoon tours in winter.

Tours are almost always full at **BAJA'S ATVS** (Blvd. Marina, behind Plaza Las Glorias, Cabo San Lucas, tel. 624/143–2050), so reserve a day in advance. Try the 9 AM or 12:30 PM departure for the lighthouse tour; the 4 PM tour is the most crowded and it returns at dark along some main roads. (ATVs kick up a lot of dust, reducing night visibility considerably.) A Candelaria trip leaves at 9 AM daily.

CABO'S MOTO RENT (Av. Cárdenas, in front of Puerto Paraíso, Cabo San Lucas, tel. 624/143–0808) has a desert tour and a beach tour at Playa Migriño on the Pacific, along with the lighthouse and Candelaria tours. ATV rentals are available. **DESERT PARK** (Cabo Real, across from Meliá Cabo Real, the Corridor, tel. 624/144–0127) leads ATV tours three times a day through the desert arroyos and canyons. The tours are more ecologically oriented than most, and guides point out geological formations and desert plants. **TIO SPORTS** (Playa Médano, Cabo San Lucas, tel. 624/143–3399) has lighthouse and Candelaria tours.

BIKING

Bicycling isn't a major activity in Los Cabos. The lack of bike paths and the dangerous road conditions make it difficult to use bikes as a mode of transportation, and the heat quickly saps your energy. Mountain bikes are available for rent from **DESERT PARK** (Cabo Real, across from Meliá Cabo Real, the Corridor, tel. 624/144–0127). Their mountain bike trails are located far from public roads. Bikes rent for $15 an hour and $50 a day.

BOAT TOURS

The themes of Los Cabos boat tours vary, but all tours follow essentially the same route: through Bahía Cabo San Lucas, past El Arco and the sea-lion colony, around Land's End into the Pacific Ocean, and then east through the Sea of Cortez along the Corridor. Costs run about $30–$40 per person; all tours include an open bar.

Winter season whale-watching in the Sea of Cortez with **CABO EXPEDITIONS** (Plaza las Glorias Hotel, Cabo San Lucas, tel. 624/143–2700) is done from small, customized, inflatable Zodiac boats that allow passengers to get close to great gray and humpback whales. At times the whales even approach the boats with their babies. Fourteen passengers are allowed per tour. The

🕐 60-foot sailboat **ENCORE** (Cabo Isla Marina near Plaza Bonita, Cabo San Lucas, tel. 624/145–8383) carries 30 passengers maximum. Whale-watching tours are offered in the morning from January to March, and sunset cruises are offered throughout the year. *Encore* tours are more sedate than those on the party boats.

The **JUNGLE CRUISE** (Plaza Las Glorias dock, Cabo San Lucas, tel. 624/143–7530) is a typical booze cruise, with loud reggae and other party music. It attracts a twenty- to thirtysomething crowd. It heads out at 6 PM and returns at 8 PM. **KALEIDOSCOPE** (marina near the Marina Fiesta hotel, Cabo San Lucas, tel. 624/148–7318) is a luxurious, 100-foot power catamaran with comfortable seating inside and out. The whale-watching tour (10 AM to 12:30 PM) and the sunset cruise (5 to 7) are geared toward couples and families.

The double-decker party boat **OCEANUS** (Blvd. Marina, below El Galeón restaurant, Cabo San Lucas, tel. 624/143–1059) has a sunset cruise with a live band. It leaves at 5 PM (6 PM in summer) from the main dock in Cabo San Lucas. **PEZ GATO** (Plaza Las Glorias dock, Cabo San Lucas, tel. 624/143–3797) has two 42-foot catamarans, *Pez Gato* I and *Pez Gato* II. You can choose the tranquil, romantic sunset cruise or the rowdier "booze cruise." Sunset cruises depart from 5 to 7; there's no romantic sailing on Tuesday. A whale-watching cruise sails daily from 10:30 AM to 1:30 PM in winter.

🕐 Cruises on the remarkable **PIRATE SHIP** (Plaza Las Glorias dock, Cabo San Lucas, tel. 624/143–4050), built in 1885, are ideal for families with children. Deckhands dressed in pirate garb let kids help hoist the sail and tie knots, while they learn about the rich history of pirates in Cabo San Lucas. There's even a working cannon on board. The whale-watching trip uses hydrophones to listen to the whales' song. The 105-foot ship can hold 150 people. It sails from 10:30 AM to 1 PM and includes hot dogs and hamburgers. The two-hour sunset cruise departs at 5 PM from Monday through Saturday. Kids under age 12 ride free.

ECOTOURISM

Ecotour prices vary, but most are $85–$100 per person.

Trips with **BAJA SALVAJE** (Obregón at Guerrero, San José del Cabo, tel. 624/142–5300, www.bajawild.com) might include hikes to canyons, small waterfalls, hot springs, a fossil-rich area, or caves with rock paintings. You can also take a customized trip to La Sierra la Laguna, a series of mountain peaks submerged in water millions of years ago. The highest peak, at 7,000 feet above sea level, is ringed by pure pine forests. Rock-climbing and rappelling trips are also available. A seven-hour day trip includes breakfast, lunch, and hotel pickup and drop-off.

★ ☺ **ECO TOURS DE BAJA** (Zaragoza at 5 de Febrero, Cabo San Lucas, tel. 624/143–0775) organizes a tour that includes a bumpy, exciting ride in a four-wheel-drive vehicle to a region rich with fossils, some millions of years old—you may even see a fossilized whale skeleton. Guides are knowledgeable and speak English. The area is protected by INAH, Mexico's National Institute of Anthropology and History, and several sites are being explored by scientists. During the ride you pass small ranches and vast fields of cardon cacti. Bird-watching is excellent early in the morning. Other tours include visits to the woodworking and leather factories in Miraflores and to waterfalls and lakes in the mountains. Trips, which cost about $60, include a barbecue lunch at a small ranch, as well as hotel pickup and drop-off.

GOLF

Los Cabos has become one of the world's top golf destinations, thanks to Fonatur, Mexico's government tourism development agency, which decided to expand Los Cabos's appeal beyond sportfishing. In 1988, it opened a 9-hole course in San José. Green fairways now appear like oases in the middle of the desert, with breathtaking holes alongside the Sea of Cortez.

Eyes in the Sky

An extraordinary variety of winged creatures color the landscape and skies of Los Cabos. Four distinct habitats—desert, ocean, pine forest, and tropical forest—afford great diversity of birds for such a small region. Cabo's location at the tip of a peninsula also makes it quite popular with migrating birds, who either stop here to rest in late autumn before venturing farther south or remain here through the winter.

Ten species of hummingbirds—including xanthus—along with the yellow-billed thrasher and yellow-footed gull are some of the more watched-for species native to the area. Other species of particular interest to bird-watchers are cactus wrens, caracara, roadrunners, brown and white pelicans, the gila woodpecker, blue-footed boobies, and the endangered peregrine falcon. The best viewing spots can be found in the Sierra de la Laguna range and the freshwater estuaries in San José and Playa Las Palmas. The best times to spot birds are just after dawn and just before sunset.

Some courses in Cabo offer memberships, but most allow nonmembers to play. The exception is Querencia, designed by Tom Fazzio. The course is said to be spectacular, but it's only open to members and their guests.

About a million gallons of water a day are required to maintain each course, which partially explains why courses charge some of the highest greens fees in the world. The cost usually includes access to the driving range, a golf cart, and bottled water. Some courses offer reduced rates for twilight play (after 3 PM). Rates given here are for high season, approximately November to May. Most hotels near the courses offer packages and reduced fees. Reservations are essential at all courses unless it's noted otherwise.

On the inland side of the Corridor, **CABO DEL SOL DESERT COURSE** (Hwy. 1, Km 10.3, the Corridor, tel. 624/145–8200, 800/386–2405 in the U.S., www.cabodelsol.com) is said to be "user-friendly": the longest hole is 625 yards, par 5. The course was designed by Tom Weiskopf. Special rates are available if you play both this and the Cabo del Sol Ocean Course. Greens fees start at $148 for twilight times, and $198 during the day.

CABO DEL SOL OCEAN COURSE (Hwy. 1, Km 10.3, the Corridor, tel. 624/145–8200, 800/386–2405 in the U.S., www.cabodelsol.com) has been included in *Golf Digest*'s "Top 100 Courses in the World." According to designer Jack Nicklaus, it has the best three finishing holes in the world. On the par-3 17th hole, you drive over an ocean inlet with waves crashing below. The 18th hole is a mirror image of the 18th at Pebble Beach, California. Six holes are seaside. Greens fees start at $170 for twilight times, and $228 during the day.

The challenging **CABO REAL GOLF COURSE** (Hwy. 1, Km 19.5, the Corridor, tel. 624/144–0040, 800/393–0400 in the U.S., www.caboreal.com), designed by Robert Trent Jones II, has straight and narrow fairways, difficult slopes, and strategically placed bunkers. The first 6 holes are in mountainous terrain, working their way up to 500 feet above sea level. Recovering from mistakes here can be quite difficult. Three holes are oceanfront. The course played host to the PGA Senior Slam in 1996 and 1999. Greens fees for 18 holes are $220, and $154 at twilight.

Renowned for spectacular views of the Sea of Cortez and El Arco—especially from the 18th hole—**RAVEN GOLF CLUB** (Hwy. 1, Km 3.6, Cabo San Lucas, tel./fax 624/143–4654, tel. 888/328–8501 in the U.S., www.intrawestgolf.com) has seven man-made lakes. The course was designed by the Dye Corporation. The signature hole is the par-5 7th. Eighteen holes are $180.

The area's original course, **CAMPO DEL GOLF SAN JOSÉ** (Hwy. 1, Km 31.5, San José del Cabo, tel. 624/142–0905), has wide fairways and few obstacles or slopes. It's good for beginners or as a warm-up. The well-maintained 9 holes are lined with residential properties (broken windows are not unusual). Some holes have nice ocean views, and there's a large lake near the bottom. It costs $54 to play 9 holes, including cart rental.

Designed by Jack Nicklaus, **EL DORADO** (Hwy. 1, Km 20, the Corridor, tel. 624/144–5451, 800/393–0400 in the U.S., www caboreal.com) is on many golf publications' top-10 lists. With 6 holes adjacent to the sea and four man-made lakes, this 18-hole course is stunning from start to finish. The fairways are wide and the greens fast. It costs $252 to play 18 holes.

The 27-hole **PALMILLA GOLF COURSE** (Hwy. 1, Km 7.5, the Corridor, tel. 624/146–7000, 954/809–2726 in the U.S.) has wide fairways, gentle slopes, and large, challenging greens. On the 10th hole, you drive from a cliff, with the sea at your back; on the famous par-4 14th, you drive onto an island fairway. One hole borders the Sea of Cortez, and 12 holes have excellent sea views. It costs $160 for Palmilla guests and $195 for nonguests to play 9 holes. You can make reservations up to 60 days in advance.

GYMS

If your hotel or resort doesn't have a gym, a few in Cabo San Lucas allow short-term memberships. Fees average about $8 a day, $25 a week, and $45 a month.

CLUB FIT (Plaza Nautica, Blvd. Marina, Cabo San Lucas, no phone) has excellent facilities, including a pool, free weights, and a variety of exercise machines. The club also has aerobics and yoga classes and a health bar. Hours are weekdays 6 AM–9:30 PM, Saturday 8–8, and Sunday 10–5. The locals work out at **GIMNASIO RUDOS** (Av. Cárdenas and Guerrero, Cabo San Lucas, tel. 624/143–0077), a basic gym with free weights and machines. There are showers for men but not for women. It's open weekdays 6 AM–10 PM, Saturday 6 AM–8 PM.

HORSEBACK RIDING

Cantering down an isolated beach or up a desert trail is one of the great pleasures of Los Cabos (as long as the sun isn't beating down too heavily). The following companies have well-fed and well-trained horses. One-hour trips generally cost about $35 per person, two-hour trips about $65.

The **CUADRA SAN FRANCISCO EQUESTRIAN CENTER** (Hwy. 1, Km 19.5, across from Cabo Real development, the Corridor, tel. 624/144–0160) gives trail rides and lessons. Its 45 beautiful show horses are well-trained. Trail rides go into the hills overlooking Cabo Real or to the San Carlos arroyo; both focus on the flora as much as the riding. Trips are limited to 20 people, with one guide for every 6 or 7 people. Reserve at least a day in advance and request an English-speaking guide. Horses are available for rent in front of the Playa Médano hotels; contact **RANCHO COLLINS HORSES** (tel. 624/143–3652). The popular **RED ROSE RIDING STABLES** (Hwy. 1, Km 4, Cabo San Lucas, tel. 624/143–4826) has healthy horses for all levels of riders. The outfitter leads trips to the beach and the desert. Groups are sometimes too large to suit all riders' levels of expertise.

ROCK CLIMBING

Three-hour trips with **BAJA SALVAJE** (Obregón at Guerrero, San José del Cabo, tel. 624/142–5300, www.bajawild.com) follow one of six routes. Four focus on rock climbing and two are dedicated to rappelling. Rock faces range from 120 feet to 320 feet, and some have extraordinary views of the ocean. Trips are designed for beginners or experts and can include as few as two people.

Until the tour van pulled up, the little roadside stand along Highway 1 had been having a slow day. As the group approached, their guide was already in conversation with the shopkeeper, who quickly brought out a small bottle of liquor. "Damiana!" he proclaimed with a grin. "A local liquor," explained the guide. "It's an aphrodisiac." Everyone scrambled to buy a bottle.

In This Chapter

By Joan Gonzalez

Updated by Maribeth Mellin

here & there

IF BASKING IN THE SUN, hauling in a record billfish, or roaring over sand dunes on an ATV become old hat, consider a leisurely day of sightseeing instead. Although Los Cabos is known more for beach- and bar-side action than for sightseeing, it nevertheless does hold its share of cultural and historic points of interest.

A day spent in either Cabo San Lucas or San José del Cabo can be a stroll that simply follows your whims, or an organized tour led by a local guide. A few tour operators run day trips through the two towns, as well as more adventurous treks through outlying areas, including the East Cape. If you would rather skip terra firma and ride the waves, boat tours from the marina in San Lucas include a pirate-ship adventure, whale-watching, and sunset cruises. Cruises can be booked through your hotel, or you can go to the Cabo San Lucas Marina before 4 PM to see what's available.

Note that some sightseeing tours lack knowledgeable guides. It is especially a problem when drivers double as guides—you are often encouraged to wander around on your own instead of being led to an interesting museum, historical site, or unusual shop. To ensure a worthwhile tour, request an itinerary beforehand and make sure everything you want to see is listed.

Numbers in the margin correspond to points of interest on the Cabos San Lucas and San José del Cabo maps.

CABO SAN LUCAS

Once an unsightly fishing town, Cabo San Lucas has become Los Cabos's tourism center. The sportfishing fleet has its

cabo san lucas

El Arco, 7

El Faro de
Cabo Falso, 8

La Parroquia de
San Lucas, 3

Mercado de
Artesanías, 4

Museo de las
Californias, 2

Plaza Bonita, 5

Plaza San Lucas, 1

Puerto Paraíso, 6

headquarters here, and cruise ships anchored off the marina discharge passengers into town. Trendy restaurants and bars line the streets, and massive hotels have risen on every available plot of waterfront turf. Bustling San Lucas elevates people-watching to a world-class sport—one that can keep you entertained for hours.

After you've wandered in and out of shops, visited the glass factory, played in the surf, and developed a ruddy glow from too much sun, it's time for some serious sightseeing. Though most of San Lucas can be seen by foot, it's worth taking a water taxi or glass-bottom boat out to El Arco (The Arch) and Playa del Amor (Lover's Beach) for a closer look.

Many restaurants and bars in this party town are more than a place to eat and drink, they are sights to see—often hysterical, not historical, and with names as whimsical as their facades. A few of these are Cabo Wabo, El Squid Roe, and the Giggling Marlin. See the Nightlife and the Arts chapter for descriptions of these multifaceted attractions.

A Good Tour

Start your walking tour from the terra-cotta–hued **PLAZA LAS GLORIAS HOTEL** on Boulevard Marina, in front of the Cabo San Lucas Marina. This sprawling hotel is impossible to miss. Head up Calle Hidalgo to Avenida Cárdenas and Plaza Amelia Wilkes, more commonly called **PLAZA SAN LUCAS** ①. This is a pleasant spot to absorb the passing scene of locals and tourists browsing in the galleries, bars, and restaurants. Stop in at the modest **MUSEO DE LAS CALIFORNIAS** ② with a giant whale skeleton out front; peruse the displays on fossils and Cabo's history. Just beyond the plaza, on Calle Cabo San Lucas between Calles Madero and Zapata, stands **LA PARROQUIA DE SAN LUCAS** ③, the town's parish church.

Walk back down Hidalgo toward the Bahía de Cabo San Lucas (Cabo San Lucas Bay) and turn right on Boulevard Marina. A walkway runs along the water's edge and the **CABO SAN LUCAS HARBOR,** where boats dock at several marinas. The traditional docks for fishing boats line the south side of the marina near the end of Boulevard Marina (though some boats now pull in on the opposite side of the bay near the Hotel Hacienda). Sportfishing boats usually start returning around 1 PM, and anglers tend to hang around bragging about their hauls. It's a rare day that a fishing boat returns empty-handed. The color of the flags flying from the boats tells you if they have caught a marlin: if it's blue, one's aboard; if red, it was caught and released. Browse through the crafts stalls near the docks at the **MERCADO DE ARTESANÍAS** ④. Vendors at the market are willing to barter over their prices, especially when there aren't any cruise ships in port.

For a cool drink and more shopping, walk north around the bay, past the Plaza Las Glorias (where some fishing and tour boats depart) to the shops and restaurants at **PLAZA BONITA** ⑤ and **PUERTO PARAÍSO** ⑥. You can snack on everything from tapas to Häagen-Dazs while surveying the private yachts and fishing boats in the marina. After refueling, continue around the bay to **PLAYA MÉDANO.** Linger to watch the beach action or take in the view of **EL ARCO** ⑦ from an open-air café.

If you have any energy left, continue your tour with a boat ride out to El Arco. Water taxis and glass-bottom boats pick up passengers at Playa Médano (or at the Cabo San Lucas Marina, if you prefer). An exhilarating way to end your day is with a sunset ride on horseback or ATV to **EL FARO DE CABO FALSO** ⑧, the remains of a 19th-century lighthouse.

TIMING

Allow a full day to take in Cabo San Lucas at a comfortable pace. If you skip the boat ride to El Arco and the trip to El Faro, then a stroll around town can be done in a half day. It's best to walk along the uphill and downhill streets between Boulevard Marina and Plaza San Lucas in the early morning or late afternoon, when it isn't so hot. When the cruise ships drop anchor, San Lucas's streets get crowded, especially during high season.

What to See

CABO SAN LUCAS HARBOR. The boot-shape harbor is the focal point for San Lucas's boating community. Many sportfishing boats pick up anglers at the docks at the south end of the marina, where water taxis and glass-bottom boats also dock. Some sportfishing companies use the marina behind the Plaza Las Glorias Hotel, which is also used by most of the large tour boats, while others depart from the marina near the Hotel Hacienda. A third marina at the north end of the harbor is filled with gorgeous private yachts. Vendors wander along the harbor walkway hawking fishing trips, sunset cruises, and, of course, time-shares.

❼ EL ARCO (The Arch). The most spectacular sight in Cabo San Lucas, this natural rock arch is visible from the marina and from some hotels, but it's most impressive from the water. If you don't take at least a short boat ride out to the Arch and Playa del Amor, the beach underneath the Arch, you haven't fully appreciated Cabo.

❽ EL FARO DE CABO FALSO (Lighthouse of the False Cape). The abandoned shell of a lighthouse built in 1890 sits amid sand dunes, some more than 500 feet high, and overlooks the cape and a 1912 shipwreck. To reach the lighthouse by land, you need an ATV, a four-wheel-drive vehicle, or a horse. A dirt road slightly north of San Lucas, off Highway 19, leads to the lighthouse and a secluded beach where turtles come ashore to lay their eggs.

❸ LA PARROQUIA DE SAN LUCAS (St. Luke's Catholic Church). The original church on this site was founded by the Jesuits in about 1740. The current church is a simple and solemn structure that's constantly being remodeled and enlarged. *Av. Cabo San Lucas, between Madero and Zapata, no phone. Daily dawn–dusk.*

④ MERCADO DE ARTESANÍAS (Crafts Market). Mexican crafts, from pottery and blankets to shawls and sombreros, are sold here. Treasures include wood carvings of marlin and whales. You can arrange a glass-bottom boat ride here. *Cabo San Lucas Marina, south end of Blvd. Marina. Daily 8 AM–9 PM.*

② MUSEO DE LAS CALIFORNIAS (Museum of the Californias). The white skeleton of an adult gray whale stretches in front of this small but growing museum dedicated to the archaeology and culture of the Baja Peninsula. Exhibits include a collection of fossils, pottery, and ranching implements. *Av. Hidalgo, across from Plaza San Lucas, tel. 624/143–0187. $1. Tues.–Sat. 8–3.*

PLAYA MÉDANO. The most popular stretch in Los Cabos for sunbathing and people-watching, this 3-km (2-mi) span of tan sand is typically crowded, especially on weekends. More active types can rent Jet Skis and sea kayaks, go parasailing, or work up a sweat jogging. After all this exercise—even if it's just your eyes that are tired from watching everyone else—relax at one of the beachfront eateries: **Mango Deck** (tel. 624/143–0901), **Billygan's Island** (tel. 624/143–4830), or the **Office** (tel. 624/143–3464).

Getting to Médano in the early morning—the only time this beach even hints at serenity—could reward you with crowds of migrating whales far offshore, especially January–April.

⑤ PLAZA BONITA. On the waterfront at the beginning of Boulevard Marina, this pretty bilevel plaza has some of the nicest shops in town. Several restaurants line its waterfront area. *Bordered by Blvd. Marina and Av. Cárdenas.*

① PLAZA SAN LUCAS. The main downtown street, Avenida Lázaro Cárdenas, passes this pretty plaza (also called Plaza Amelia Wilkes) with a white wrought-iron gazebo. The center of the tourist part of town, it is surrounded by shops and restaurants.

⑥ PUERTO PARAÍSO. The view of the marina has forever been changed by this enormous, elegant complex, which will eventually include a shopping mall, hotels, condos, a spa, and a convention center. At this writing, the shopping mall is open and filling with franchise restaurants (Johnny Rockets, Ruth's Chris Steak House, Häagen-Dazs) and boutiques hawking sportswear, jewelry, and souvenirs. *Av. Cárdenas at Blvd. Marina, tel. 624/143–0000.*

SAN JOSÉ DEL CABO

The municipal headquarters for Los Cabos, San José has a population of about 25,000. The hotel zone is on a long stretch of waterfront facing the Sea of Cortez; a 9-hole golf course and a private residential community have been established south of town center. The downtown area, with its adobe houses and jacaranda trees, still maintains the languid pace of a Mexican village, though bumper-to-bumper traffic sometimes clogs the streets during weekday business hours. Despite recent hotel development, San José remains the more peaceful of the Los Cabos towns—the one to come to for a quiet escape.

Hotels along the Paseo Malecón San José (the coastal strip between where Highway 1 curves north and the Paseo Malecón ends, at the Hotel Presidente Inter-Continental) are about a 15-minute walk from most restaurants and shops. A taxi from the hotels to downtown costs about $6 each way. There's a taxi stand on Boulevard Mijares near Plaza Mijares. If you're staying in San Lucas or the Corridor and want to explore the San José area, you may want to rent a car. Parking is usually available around the town center.

A Good Tour

Driving in from San Lucas or the Corridor, follow Paseo Malecón San José to **BOULEVARD MIJARES** ⑨ and park near **PLAZA MIJARES** ⑩. A good choice for lunch is the Damiana Restaurant, housed in an 18th-century house off the northeast corner of the plaza. You can eat outside under a tree, inside surrounded by antiques, or on the back patio amid flowering bougainvillea. Linger over lunch, as some shops close from noon to 2 PM.

After a relaxing lunch, set out to explore San José on foot. It's impossible to get lost in this easy walking town: simply look up for the church's twin spires, visible from any point, and you'll have found the main plaza. The length of your walk will depend on how much time you spend in the shops. Stop in first at the **IGLESIA SAN JOSÉ** ⑪ on Zaragoza at Morelos. Walk east along Zaragoza, visiting the shops surrounding the plaza, and head south down Boulevard Mijares. At the corner of Avenida Manuel Doblado is **EL PALACIO MUNICIPAL** ⑫, which you can recognize by its clock tower. Continue as far as you like along Boulevard Mijares; then cross to the other side and work your way back to the plaza. At the far end of the boulevard, past many intriguing shops, is the **CASA DE LA CULTURA** ⑬. If you're thirsty from your walk, stop next door for a drink in the lovely courtyard of the Casa Natalia hotel. Several excellent restaurants and a few galleries line the streets just north of the plaza. This neighborhood is worth exploring for new discoveries.

TIMING
Unless you want to devote a lot of time to shopping, the town of San José can easily be seen in a half day and can be paired with a side trip to **SANTIAGO** (☞ Off the Beaten Path, *below*). To avoid driving after dark, go to Santiago first, returning to explore San José in the late afternoon and/or early evening.

What to See

⑨ **BOULEVARD MIJARES.** The main street in San José del Cabo, Mijares is lined with restaurants and shops; the fountain in the center median is illuminated at night. The south end of the boulevard has been designated the tourist zone, with the Los Cabos Club de Golf as its centerpiece. The boulevard ends at Paseo Malecón San José, where a few reasonably priced hotels and

san josé del cabo

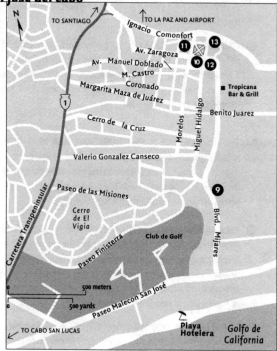

N

TO SANTIAGO ↑TO LA PAZ AND AIRPORT

Ignacio Comonfort

Av. Zaragoza **11** **13**

Av. Manuel Doblado **10** **12**

M. Castro

Coronado ■ Tropicana
Bar & Grill

Margarita Maza de Juárez

Cerro de la Cruz

Valerio Gonzalez Canseco

Paseo de las Misiones

Cerro
de El
Vigia Club de Golf

Paseo Finisterra

Morelos

Miguel Hidalgo

Benito Juarez

Blvd. Mijares

9

Carretera Transpeninsular

0 500 meters

0 500 yards

Paseo Malecón San José

TO CABO SAN LUCAS

Playa
Hotelera Golfo de
California

Boulevard
Mijares, 9

Casa de la
Cultura, 13

Iglesia
San José, 11

El Palacio
Municipal, 12

Plaza Mijares, 10

large all-inclusive resorts face a beautiful, long stretch of beach that's perfect for morning strolls (the surf, unfortunately, is too rough for swimming).

13 CASA DE LA CULTURA (House of Culture). During the 1847 War of Intervention, this simple terra-cotta–color building served as a refuge for a company of American sailors. It now occasionally hosts theater, music, and dance performances. *Blvd. Mijares and Obregón, no phone. Mon.–Sat. 9–8.*

NEED A BREAK? The sidewalk café at the **TROPICANA BAR AND GRILL** (Blvd. Mijares 30, tel. 624/142–1580), near Plaza Mijares, is a favorite tourist hangout. Walk around to the back to see the gardens and the lovely indoor restaurant. It was once a 19th-century home, as were many of the buildings in San José del Cabo.

11 IGLESIA SAN JOSÉ. The town's twin-spired 1940 church looms above Plaza Mijares. This was originally the site of a Jesuit mission erected in 1735, one year after Pericú Indians decapitated the Jesuit priest Father Nicolás Tamaral. A tile mural over the church entrance shows him being dragged toward a raging fire. *Zaragoza at Morelos, no phone. Daily dawn–dusk.*

12 EL PALACIO MUNICIPAL (City Hall). Built in 1891, this modest yellow-and-white building near Plaza Mijares has a conspicuous clock tower. *Blvd. Mijares and Zaragoza, no phone. Weekdays 9–5.*

10 PLAZA MIJARES. Locals and travelers mingle at the central plaza, where a wrought-iron gazebo and forest-green benches are set in the shade. There's a small stage and space for art shows and celebrations. *Bounded by Blvd. Mijares, Hidalgo, Obregón, and Zaragoza.*

SANTIAGO. This small ranching and farming town (population 2,500), settled by the Jesuits in 1724, is 52 km (32 mi) north of San José del Cabo—about a one-hour drive. Turn off Highway 1 at Km 84, just north of the large cement ball that marks the line of the Tropic of Cancer. You should soon see orchards as well as vegetable and sugarcane fields, before arriving at Santiago's town square surrounded by old adobe homes.

Calle Guadalupe Victoria, the main street that takes you to the town plaza, will bring you past several sights. The **Parque Zoológico Santiago** (Santiago Zoo; Calle Guadalupe Victoria s/n, no phone), open daily 6–6, serves as a sanctuary for animals and birds that have been injured and can no longer survive in the wild. The modest zoo doesn't charge admission, but donations are appreciated. On the corner of Calzada Maestros Misioneros de 1930 and Calle Victoria is the town's twin-spired Catholic church, erected in 1735 and since rebuilt. Next to the church is Santiago's small museum (no phone), open daily 8–1; its main attractions are fossils of giant clams, reptiles, fish, and turtles—all inhabitants of the area millions of years ago when the entire peninsula was underwater.

For a leisurely lunch, the restaurant in the garden of the rustic **Palomar Hotel** (Calzada Maestros Misioneros de 1930, no phone, no credit cards) is the perfect spot. Just outside Santiago are three **hot springs**—El Chorro, Santa Rita, and Agua Caliente—where you can relax and rejuvenate in a pool large enough to seat 25 people. To get to the hot springs, stay west on Calle Victoria (it turns into a dirt road) for about 7 km (4 mi). About 45 minutes northwest of Santiago along Calle Victoria (at this point a dirt road) is an **Indian rock-art site,** a massive exposed boulder bearing rare, dramatic "handprint" artwork.

His hair was a little long, 1970s-style; her tie-dye halter skimmed the waistband of her jeans. They were in Todos Santos, across from the Hotel California, buying up caps and T-shirts emblazoned with its logo. Hadn't they heard? This wasn't really the hotel where Don Henley holed up to write the lyrics for the Eagles' hit song of the same name. But no matter—the couple strolled across the street to the mission and exchanged knowing glances.

In This Chapter

By Joan Gonzalez

Revised by Maribeth Mellin

side trips

A CHANGE OF SCENERY can be welcome after a few days of sun worshipping, beachcombing, and tequila tasting in Los Cabos. If you're venturing out just for the day, tranquil **TODOS SANTOS, LA PAZ,** and the **EAST CAPE** are easy side trips. The first two carve different slices of Baja culture: one is a small village centered on the arts; the other is Baja Sur's bustling capital. If natural wonders are more to your taste, the East Cape, including the small communities of Buena Vista and Los Barriles, can satisfy with secluded coves and beautiful vistas.

Whether you rent a car or jeep, take a guided tour, or hop on the bus depends largely on where you want to go. The comfortable (air-conditioned and restroom–equipped) bus makes your journey relatively carefree, but if you like to explore along the way, renting a car allows you more freedom. Do not drive on the highways after dark, as there are no fences to keep animals off the roads and dips in the roads sometimes flood.

If you'd like to spend some serious time away from the tourist mecca of Los Cabos, there are a number of places to stay the night in Todos Santos, La Paz, and the East Cape (☞ Where to Stay), including the Hotel California, Todos Santos Inn, and Posada la Poza in Todos Santos; el ángel azul and La Concha Beach Resort in La Paz; and Hotel Buena Vista and Hotel Palmas de Cortez in the East Cape.

TODOS SANTOS

72 km (45 mi) north of Cabo San Lucas.

For nearly 100 years, Todos Santos was the sweetest town in Baja Sur, with sugarcane mills turning thick cane stalks into dark brown sugar. After World War II, sugar prices dropped, a severe drought and over-irrigation drained the underground springs, and mills were forced to close. Todos Santos—with its lovely adobe-and-brick homes, beautiful but windy Pacific coastline, and La Laguna mountain range as a backdrop—just went to sleep. The drought lasted 30 years. Then, in 1981, the rain poured down, the springs were revived, and Todos Santos once again became a fertile oasis.

Soon thereafter the paving of Highway 19 brought gradual progress and prosperity to the area. In recent years, Todos Santos has captured the imaginations of painters, sculptors, jewelers, and other artists. Galleries and studios come and go in Todos Santos, but there are always several worth checking out. The Todos Santos Fiesta del Arte, an art show held in February, attracts international collectors. The area is also a haven for retired Americans and those seeking a quiet way of life. Of the 5,000 inhabitants, more than 500 are Americans.

Sights to See

For the better part of the journey from Cabo San Lucas on Highway 19, all you see is ocean, tangled brush, cactus, and signs for new housing developments. Then trees and flaming bougainvillea appear, followed by rows of small houses and fields lush with leafy vegetables and clusters of palms. This is **EL PESCADERO**—the largest settlement before Todos Santos—populated by farmers who grow herbs and vegetables for restaurants in Los Cabos.

The village of Todos Santos is a small gem, with shops, art galleries, and restaurants dotting a six-block area that fans out from the church overlooking a small plaza. (At the other end of the plaza are the municipal and police offices.) Most shops and galleries are open daily 10 to 5, although hours tend to be erratic; restaurants serve mainly lunch and dinner. Some spots close for siesta; some close from late September through mid-October. In October, the Fiesta Todos Santos takes place in the days surrounding the October 12 Fiesta de la Virgen del Pilar (Feast of the Virgin of Pilar), honoring the town's patron saint. If you have a car, you can continue your drive north of Todos Santos on Highway 19 and pick up some homemade candy at the stands just outside town.

For a list of galleries, current art shows, and other happenings in town, pick up a copy of the free *El Calendario de Todos Santos* (published eight times a year) at almost any shop.

THE CHARLES STEWART GALLERY & STUDIO. Stewart moved from Taos, New Mexico, to Todos Santos in 1986 and is credited as one of the founders of the town's artistic community. Some of his paintings and art pieces have a Baja or Mexican theme. His studio is one of the loveliest 19th-century buildings in town. *Calle Centenario at Calle Obregón, tel. 612/145–0265. Daily 10–4.*

GALERÍA DE TODOS SANTOS. This corner gallery, owned by Michael and Pat Cope, displays Michael's modern art and exhibits works by international artists living in Baja. The gallery is one of the focal points for the ever-changing local arts scene. *Calle Topete and Calle Legaspi, tel. 612/145–0040. Daily 10–5.*

GALERÍA SANTA FÉ. In an 1850s adobe building across from the town's church plaza, Paula and Ezio Colombo sell original collector-quality Mexican folk art. The eclectic mix includes frames adorned with images of Frida Kahlo and her art, kid-size chairs decorated with bottle caps, Virgin of Guadalupe images, and *milagros* (small tin charms used as offerings to saints). *Calle Centenario 4, tel. 612/145–0340. Mon. and Wed–Sun. 10–5.*

Drivers Beware

Despite a paucity of traffic lights, the small towns of Baja California Sur (outside Los Cabos) are small enough that vehicular traffic is typically not a problem. Indeed, during high season, pedestrians are usually more bothersome than cars.

The greatest road hazards are cows, sudden potholes, dips (vados), and roadwork, which make it dangerous to drive after dark. Even during daylight hours, narrow roads and open ranges that allow cattle to wander where they please can be dangerous. En route to Todos Santos and La Paz, crosses and flowers at accident sites are grim reminders that fatalities on the road are all too frequent.

Stick to posted speed limits, usually 90 kph (55 mph) on the highways and 40 kph (25 mph) in town (signs are always posted in kilometers and in Spanish). Pemex service stations are abundant, but it's a good idea to keep your gas tank at least half full.

HOTEL CALIFORNIA. This hotel with a famous name is now a sophisticated inn, restaurant, and shop—all worth checking out, even though the 1970s Eagles' song of the same name has no connection to the place. The building's interior was gutted and remodeled with ochre, lavender, and grey walls and brick-and wood-beam ceilings. Public spaces are filled with antiques from around the world, and the enormous shop is a veritable international gallery. *Calle Juárez at Morelos, tel. 612/145–0525. Shop daily 10–5.*

MISIÓN DE NUESTRA SEÑORA DEL PILAR (Mission of Our Lady of Pilar). Todos Santos had brief status as a mission in the mid-1700s, but for most of that era it was a visiting mission, where *padres* (fathers) stopped briefly during their rounds of rural communities. The modest church has a few stained-glass windows. There's a nice unobstructed view of the rippling hills between the town and the ocean from the church grounds. *Calle Márquez de León, between Calle Legaspi and Calle Centenario, no phone. Free. Daily 8 AM–end of 7:30 PM mass.*

Dining

\$\$–\$\$\$ CAFÉ SANTA FÉ. Owners Paula and Ezio Colombo's Italian restaurant was one of the first upscale ventures in Todos Santos and has long drawn devotees from Los Cabos. With tables in an overgrown courtyard, the setting is part of the appeal, but the highlight is the food—salads and soups made from organic vegetables, homemade pastas, and fresh fish with light herbal sauces. The marinated seafood salad is a sublime garlicky blend of shrimp, octopus, and mussels; it makes an ample starter for two before moving on to the lobster ravioli. *Calle Centenario 4, tel. 612/145–0340. No credit cards. Closed Tues. and parts of Sept. and Oct.*

\$\$ LOS ADOBES. Palo verde trees shade diners in the courtyard behind century-old adobe houses at this serene restaurant. The menu leans toward Mexican haute cuisine, but has plenty of familiar dishes, including excellent beef fajitas. For something different, try the vegetarian *chiles rellenos* (ancho chile peppers stuffed with potatoes), or chicken with mole sauce. The Internet café beside the restaurant is a welcome addition to the town's services. *Calle Hidalgo between Calle Juárez and Calle Militar, tel. 612/145–0203. MC, V. No dinner Sun.*

\$–\$\$ CAFFÉ TODOS SANTOS. Omelets, bagels, granola, and pancakes delight the breakfast crowd at this small café. Later in the day, salads and deli sandwiches are served. Check for fresh seafood on the daily specials board and pick up a loaf of bread for the road. You can eat inexpensively here, but the menu might make you want to splurge. *Calle Centenario 33, tel. 612/145–0300. MC, V.*

\$–\$\$ MI COSTA. Locals crave the shrimp with garlic and oil served at this cement-floor *palapa* (palm thatch) café. On Sunday, families fill the dining area and feast on shrimp, fish tacos, and grilled fish fillets. Everything is Mexican casual—feel free to fetch your own napkins and condiments. *Calle Militar at Calle Ocampo, no phone. No credit cards.*

Shopping

The shopping scene is limited in Todos Santos, but the selection is excellent. **FÉNIX DE TODOS SANTOS** (Calle Juárez at Calle Topete, tel. 612/145–0666) displays bowls and plates from Tonalá, on the mainland. The unusual pottery is crafted following an ancient Japanese form of ceramics called raku. Handblown glassware, Talavera pottery, cotton clothing by the designer Sucesos, and an ever-changing display make this a fascinating place to browse.

Filled with gorgeous Guatemalan textiles, Mexican folk art, wood carvings and Day of the Dead figurines, **MANGOS** (Calle Centenario across from Charles Stewart Gallery, tel. 612/145–0451) is one of the area's most intriguing shops.

The best bookstore in the region is **EL TECOLOTE BOOKSTORE** (Calle Juárez at Calle Hidalgo, tel. 612/145–0295). Stop here for an exceptional collection of Latin American literature, poetry, children's books, current fiction and nonfiction, and books on Baja. Both English and Spanish editions, new and used, are sold, along with maps, magazines, newspapers, cards, and art supplies.

Coming & Going

Whether you're driving or taking the local bus, the best route to Todos Santos is Highway 19, traveling along the Pacific Ocean from Cabo San Lucas. Linking Todos Santos with the rest of the Baja Peninsula, the road narrows from four lanes to two at times, and goes up and down like a mild roller coaster.

BY BUS

Águila buses depart the **CABO SAN LUCAS BUS STATION** (Calle 5 de Febrero, at Carretera Todos Santos, tel. 624/143–7878) every hour. The trip takes about 90 minutes. In Todos Santos, the bus stops at open-air Pilar's Fresh Fish Tacos restaurant. Drivers don't make announcements. Return buses leave every hour from across the street; the last one usually departs at 7 PM, but be sure to ask, since the schedule changes. Bus fare is $4 each way, paid in pesos or U.S. dollars at the station in San Lucas and on the bus.

BY CAR

The trip to Todos Santos takes about an hour by car. A sign points the way to Highway 19 from Highway 1 north of San Lucas. The sign reads CARRETERA A TODOS SANTOS; follow this road to the first major intersection, and then turn right. Don't drive on the highway at night, and don't explore dirt roads off the highway unless you're in a four-wheel-drive vehicle; if you aren't, getting stuck in the sand is a strong possibility. Most streets in the center of Todos Santos have no-parking signs; look for space on side streets.

BY VAN TOUR

Full-day van tours from Los Cabos to Todos Santos cost about $65 per person including breakfast, snacks, and drinks. **CONTACTOURS** (Av. Zaragoza at 5 de Febrero, San José del Cabo, tel. 624/143–2439) will provide a van and guide for private tours. **RANCHO TOURS** (Libertad, at 20 de Noviembre, Cabo San Lucas, tel. 624/143–5464) also has full-day van tours. **TRANSCABO TOURS** (Hwy. 1, Km 43 San José del Cabo, tel. 624/146–0888) offers tours to Todos Santos.

Getting Around

The village center of Todos Santos is compact enough for you to get around on foot.

Old Baja & New

The Baja of yesteryear had two faces. One was of the upscale resort where celebrities hid out, having flown down—usually from California—in private planes; the other was of a parade of "trailers," aluminum boxes barely big enough for two people. Free spirits drove these homes-on-wheels throughout Baja California, camping overnight in trailer parks along the way. They came to commune with like-minded souls, seek oneness with nature, and just "be" in the remote beauty of southern Baja.

Times have changed, with the Baja-bound landing somewhere between the extremes of yesteryear. Trailer parks still exist, but today's sophisticated offspring come complete with power hookups and enjoy the luxuries of restaurants and nightly entertainment. Those aluminum boxes have given way to modern recreational vehicles, some larger and more luxurious than two-bedroom apartments. And instead of celebrities descending in private planes, today people from all walks of life pour off some 30 commercial flights a day into the San José International Airport.

LA PAZ

214 km (133 mi) north of San José del Cabo, 217 km (135 mi) north of Cabo San Lucas.

The capital of Baja California Sur, La Paz is a traditional city of 250,000 people, with a large contingent of retirees from the United States and Canada. The city has the feel of a mainland community that has adapted to tourism while retaining its character.

Hernán Cortés and his soldiers were drawn to La Paz in 1535 by stories of beautiful women and of oysters hiding magnificent pearls. In 1720 the Jesuits arrived to deliver their message of salvation. Instead, they inadvertently introduced smallpox, which decimated the local populace within 30 years.

A permanent settlement was established here in 1811. La Paz became the capital of the Californias in 1829 after a hurricane nearly leveled the former capital, Loreto. In 1853 a group of U.S. Southerners, led by William Walker, tried to turn La Paz into a slave state, but Mexicans quickly banished them. Nearly a century later, disease wiped out the oyster beds, leaving La Paz much less attractive to prospectors.

La Paz officially became the capital of Baja California Sur in 1974. Today its biggest asset is the Sea of Cortez—which Jacques Cousteau described as "a marine aquarium with the largest diversity of sea life we can find on Earth." La Paz is also the site of the governor's house and the state's bureaucracy, jail, and power plant, as well as the ferry port to Mazatlán.

The **tourist information center** (☎ 612/124-0100) is along Malecón Alvaro Obregón between Calles Rosales and Allende, five blocks west of the Malecón Plaza.

Sights to See

MALECÓN. The 5-km (3-mi) *malecón* (waterfront) runs along the edge of the bay near downtown. It's one of Mexico's most pleasant urban waterfronts, with playgrounds, park benches, beaches, and casual restaurants on the sand. Sprawling inland from the waterfront is southern Baja's busiest downtown, with shops crammed together on narrow streets. As you enter town from the southwest, Paseo Alvaro Obregón turns into the malecón at a cluster of high-rise condos. **Marina La Paz,** at the southwest end of the malecón, is a development with condominiums, vacation homes, and a pleasant walkway lined with casual cafés. Northeast of town, the malecón becomes what is commonly known as the **Pichilingue Road.** The road curves northeast along Bahía de la Paz (La Paz Bay) about 16 km (10 mi) to the terminals where the ferries from Mazatlán and Topolobampo arrive and many of the sportfishing boats depart.

🕙 **MALECÓN PLAZA.** A two-story white gazebo is the focus of this small paved square where musicians sometimes appear on weekend nights.

ZÓCALO. The central plaza, which also goes by the names **Plaza Constitución** and **Jardín Velazco,** is bordered by Calles Revolución, Cinco de Mayo, Independencia, and Madero.

LA CATEDRAL DE NUESTRA SEÑORA DE LA PAZ (Our Lady of La Paz Cathedral). Rising above the *zócalo* (main square), this church was built in 1860 near the site of La Paz's first mission, established that same year by Jesuit Jaime Bravo. *Calle Revolución, no phone. Daily 7 AM–8 PM.*

🕙 **MUSEO DE ANTROPOLOGÍA** (Museum of Anthropology). Baja's culture and heritage are well represented here, with re-creations of Comondú and Las Palmas Indian villages, photos of cave paintings found in Baja, and copies of Cortés's writings on first sighting La Paz. Many exhibit descriptions are written only in Spanish, but the museum staff will help you translate. A bookstore and gift shop sell ceramic pieces and replicas of Aztec, Toltec, and other pre-Columbian artworks. *Calle Altamirano and Calle Cinco de Mayo, tel./fax 612/122–0162. Donations accepted. Daily 9–6.*

PICHILINGUE. Since the time of pirate ships and Spanish invaders, this part of the bay (about 17 km [10 mi] north of La Paz) was known for its preponderance of oysters bearing black pearls. In the 1940s an unknown disease killed off the oysters, but today, Pichilingue is a pleasant place for sunbathing and for watching the sportfishing boats bringing in their hauls. Palapa restaurants on the beach serve cold beer, oysters *diablo* (raw oysters steeped in a fiery-hot sauce), and fresh grilled fish.

Dining

$–$$ LA PAZTA. Locals who crave international cuisine rave about this trattoria with a sleek, black-and-white interior and excellent homemade pasta. Imported cheeses and wines, fresh herbs and vegetables, and invigorating espresso and cappuccino are refreshing changes from the local seafood and taco fare. *Calle Allende 36, tel. 612/125–1195. MC, V.*

¢–$ **EL QUINTO SOL RESTAURANTE VEGETARIANO.** El Quinto's brightly painted exterior is covered with snake symbols and smiling suns. The all-vegetarian menu includes fresh juices and herbal elixirs. The four-course *comida corrida* (daily special) is a bargain; it's served from noon to 4. The back half of the space is a bare-bones natural-foods store. *Belisario Domínguez and Av. Independencia, tel. 612/122–1692. No credit cards.*

¢ **TACO HERMANOS GONZALEZ.** La Paz has plenty of great taco stands, but the Gonzalez brothers still corner the market with their shrimp, lobster, and hunks of fresh fish wrapped in corn tortillas. Bowls of condiments line the small stand, and the best fast food in town draws crowds of sidewalk munchers. *Calle Mutualismo and Calle Esquerro, no phone. No credit cards.*

Shopping

Locals head to "the big city" for household items, car parts, clothing, groceries, and other daily necessities, since the prices are lower and the selection larger. For folk art, check out the masks, lacquerware, and pottery (and books, too) at **ARTESANÍAS LA ANTIGUA CALIFORNIA** (Obregón 220, tel. 612/ 125–5230). **ARTESANÍA CUAUHTÉMOC** (Av. Abasolo, between Calles Nayarit and Oaxaca, no phone) is the workshop of weaver Fortunado Silva, who creates and sells cotton place mats, rugs, and tapestries. Julio Ibarra oversees the potters and painters at **IBARRA'S POTTERY** (Calle Prieto 625, tel. 612/122–0404). His geometric designs and glazing technique result in gorgeous mirrors, bowls, platters, and cups. **MEXICAN DESIGNS** (Calle Arreola 41, at Av. Zaragoza, no phone) has unusual pottery, such as ceramic boxes with cactus designs.

Coming & Going

From either Cabo San Lucas or San José del Cabo, La Paz is more than a two-hour drive, part of it through the mountains. It makes a nice day tour, as long as you don't spend too much time getting here and back. If you want to make lengthy stops, plan to spend the night (☞ Where to Stay).

BY BUS

ABC and Águila buses arrive at the **MAIN BUS STATION** (Calle Jalisco at Calle Héroes de la Independencia, tel. 612/122–4270), a 30-minute walk or a $2.50 taxi ride from downtown. **ÁGUILA** (tel. 612/122–7898) has a stop at the north end of the malecón. Buses depart the Cabo San Lucas terminal for La Paz daily, every one to two hours, traveling via Todos Santos; the fare is $10 one-way. Buses from San José del Cabo leave from the Águila terminal just off Highway 1 and pass Buena Vista and Los Barriles; the fare to La Paz is $10.

BY CAR

From San José del Cabo, take the Transpeninsular Highway (Hwy. 1). From San Lucas take Highway 19, which joins Highway 1 after Todos Santos. Or, better yet, drive up on scenic Highway 1 and back on Highway 19. Stay on the paved highways; roads are narrow and without lights, and cows and other animals roam freely. You may have to stop for road repairs during and after the rainy season.

BY VAN TOUR

Full-day van tours from Los Cabos to La Paz cost about $75 per person, including breakfast, snacks, and drinks. Ask for an itinerary beforehand, as some guides simply drop you off on the malecón and pick you up about three hours later. **CONTACTOURS** (Av. Zaragoza at 5 de Febrero, San José del Cabo, tel. 624/143–2439) will provide a van and guide for private tours to La Paz. **RANCHO TOURS** (Libertad, at 20 de Noviembre, Cabo San Lucas, tel. 624/143–5464) also has full-day van tours to La Paz. **TRANSCABO TOURS** (Hwy. 1, Km 43, San José del Cabo, tel. 624/146–0888) has tours to La Paz.

Getting Around

To get to downtown La Paz from the main bus station, take any city bus and get off at the city market, or *mercado municipal* (Calle Revolución at Calle Degollado). To return, downtown city buses marked IMSS will let you off three blocks from the terminal.

Águila buses to the beaches and ferry terminal in Pichilingue (10 a day, 20 minutes, $1) leave from **TERMINAL MALECÓN** (Av. Obregón, tel. 612/122–7898). The last bus back to La Paz departs Pichilingue at 6 PM.

BUENA VISTA & LOS BARRILES
Buena Vista: 32 km (20 mi) north of San José del Cabo; Los Barriles: 34 km (21 mi) north of San José del Cabo.

The Sea of Cortez coast between La Paz and San José del Cabo is a favored hideaway for anglers and adventurers. The area by San José, dubbed the East Cape, consists of several fast-growing settlements including Cabo Pulmo, Buena Vista, Los Barriles, and Punta Pescadero. The East Cape is renowned for its rich fishing grounds, good diving, and excellent windsurfing. Most hotels (☞ Where to Stay) offer packages that include meals and activities. The East Cape makes a good day trip or a nice place to overnight, especially if you're into water sports.

Intrepid travelers can drive north on a dirt washboard road to the East Cape settlements, then return on the paved Highway 1. This route is not recommended for those bothered by dust or long stretches of precipitous driving conditions; some car rental agencies do not allow their cars on these roads. Stop along the way to snorkel or dive in Cabo Pulmo or windsurf in Los Barriles. If you want to fish this part of the Sea of Cortez, plan on spending a night so you can be out on the water in early morning. You can rent water-sports equipment and organize boat trips through area hotels.

Sights to See

The East Cape is more about activities than attractions. Whether you drive the dirt road or highway, you'll find plenty of places to stop and play or simply admire the scenery. The following places are worth exploring as you work your way north from San José.

Divers and snorkelers need go no farther than **CABO PULMO**, site of one of the few coral reefs in the Sea of Cortez. You can dive with one of the shops in the area or just snorkel and swim about admiring the tropical fish. The reef is part of a national marine reserve, and you may not remove anything from the water. Rustic stands on the beach sell food and drinks.

Vacationers and expat settlers are drawn to **BUENA VISTA**, which has more services and infrastructure than the East Cape's more remote outposts. You can sign up for fishing and diving excursions at the Hotel Buena Vista Beach Resort.

Atop the flat crest of La Bandera mountain stands an elaborate, towering **CONCRETE FLAGPOLE**. The memorial honors Mexico's flag and is the site of the Día de la Bandera (Day of the Flag) fiesta, which takes place February 24. The fiesta emerged as a kind of cultural-pride response to the growing American influence in the area in the 1950s. To reach the memorial, take the dirt road that winds up through the rocks near the Buena Vista turnoff from Highway 1.

La Bandera mountain affords spectacular views of **BAHÍA DE PALMAS** (Bay of Palms), one of the most beautiful coves on the Sea of Cortez. Many of the East Cape's resorts face the bay. Windsurfers are drawn by the fierce winds during the winter months. **Vela Windsurf** (tel. 800/223–5443 in the U.S., www.velawindsurf.com) arranges multiday windsurfing trips based at East Cape hotels from November through mid-March. Las

Palmas Bay is 77 km (48 mi) north of San José on Highway 1; turn off at the Buena Vista sign.

Dining

$–$$ **OTRA VEZ.** If you're ready for grilled fish or a burger by the time you reach Los Barriles, stop at this great little California-style café. The clientele consists largely of expat retirees and tourists who gossip freely while listening to the Beach Boys or occasional live music. *Calle 20 de Noviembre, Los Barriles, tel. 612/142–0249. MC, V.*

¢–$ **TIA LICHA.** A good, solid place to start your day is at this tiny café known for its home-style cooking and fresh fish. Locals congregate here for what is said to be the best breakfast on the East Cape. *On the road to Hotel Buena Vista Beach Resort, Buena Vista, no phone. No credit cards.*

Coming & Going

Along Highway 1, Buena Vista is 75 km (47 mi) and Los Barriles 77 km (48 mi) north of San José. Travel during the week if possible, as weekends can be crowded.

The simplest way to visit these neighboring towns in one day is to rent a car. You can reach several beaches easily, but to navigate most dirt roads safely—including the rough Coastal Road—you need a four-wheel-drive vehicle with high ground clearance. Get a good map that shows off-road routes. The cape's more courteous drivers turn on their left-turn signal to indicate that you may pass them. Watch closely, though. The driver may actually be turning left.

You can also arrange van tours to the East Cape from Los Cabos. Prices run about $65 for a full-day van tour. **RANCHO TOURS** (Libertad, at 20 de Noviembre, Cabo San Lucas, tel. 624/143–5464) offers ATV tours on the East Cape; call for details and prices. **TRANSCABO TOURS** (Hwy. 1, Km 43, San José del Cabo, tel. 624/146–0888) runs van tours to Cabo Pulmo.

Music pumped out of enormous speakers as the emcee screamed, "Get crazy!" All around her, sun-red partyers chugged beers and slurped Jell-O shots, dancing waiters wove in and out around belly-baring women grinding with muscle-bound men on the dance floor—while a large stuffed bear looked on. A hand beckoned her from the writhing crowd. She hesitated, then crossed over, thinking, "So this is why they call it Cabo San Loco."

In This Chapter

By Brad Weiss

Revised and Updated by Maribeth Mellin

nightlife & the arts

PARTY-MINDED CROWDS ROAM the main strip of Cabo San Lucas every night from happy hour through late-night dancing—often staggering home or to their hotel rooms just before dawn. It's not hard to see why this is the nightlife capital of southern Baja. Indeed, San Lucas is internationally famous (or infamous, depending on your view) for being a raucous party town, especially during Spring Break. Most of the nightlife is focused on bars and dance clubs, where a very lively pickup scene predominates. Beware the tequila shooters and Jell-O shots forced upon revelers by merry waiters—they cost at least $5 each. Topless bars and "gentleman's" clubs are abundant, too. Single men are often accosted outside San Lucas bars with offers for drugs and sex, but beware—you could be falling into a police trap.

After-dark action in San José del Cabo caters mostly to locals and tourists seeking tranquillity and seclusion. What little nightlife there is revolves around restaurants, casual bars, and large hotels—coming to life on Thursday and going back to sleep Sunday. There are no big dance clubs or discos in San José (though in this fast-changing scene, something may open by the time you visit).

Between the two towns, the self-contained resorts along the Corridor have no nightlife to speak of. Only resort guests frequent the hotel bars, and the sunset-watching crowd departs soon after darkness descends. If you want to dance the night away, stay in Cabo San Lucas.

For years Todos Santos has been the bohemian center of southern Baja, and Los Cabos has concerned itself with partying. But Los Cabos now has a fledgling arts scene. A few galleries and talented artists in Cabo San Lucas brave the party scene and open studios. Some Los Cabos hotels hold special art events, during which prominent local artists, often with international reputations, exhibit their works and meet the public.

Cabo's first annual jazz festival was held in July 2003, and organizers say they will continue presenting the festival, though no dates are set. There's also a Baja Reggae Fest at San Pedrito (between Cabo San Lucas and Todos Santos) usually held in February.

Classical music and dance performances remain few and far between. If you're looking for music, stop by the Puerto Paraíso mall in Cabo San Lucas starting around 5 PM or 7 PM, when you might find folkloric dance performances by the marina or jazz concerts in the Japanese garden area. At the Solmar Suites hotel in Cabo San Lucas (tel. 624/143-3535), a Mexican Fiesta with a buffet dinner, folkloric dance show, and games is held every Saturday night. Fortunately there has been an increasing interest in the history and culture of Baja, which may lead to a richer artistic environment, with more events such as these, in the years to come.

How & When

Bars and clubs in San José del Cabo and Cabo San Lucas don't usually have cover charges unless a well-known group is playing. Many don't even open until 10 PM. Closing times are determined by specific government licenses and vary greatly; the latest is 5:30 AM. The drinking age in Mexico is 18, but it's not strictly enforced.

Waking the Dead

Celebrated throughout Mexico, the most important religious and indigenous festival in Los Cabos takes place November 1 and 2: All Saints' and All Souls' Day, more commonly referred to as **DÍA DE LOS MUERTOS** (Day of the Dead). Long before Spain conquered Mexico, the festival was part of Indian culture and held during the winter equinox. In true colonial spirit, Spain changed the timing to coincide with its religious All Saints' and All Souls' Day.

Not as macabre as it sounds, the festival is a joyous celebration to welcome a visit from the souls of deceased loved ones. Family and friends prepare favorite foods and drink of the dearly departed, burn candles and incense, and place flowers in cemeteries and at memorials along the road. Shops carry candy shaped like skulls and coffins, and bread is baked to look like ghosts. No tears are to be shed, as it is said that the path back to the living world must not be made slippery by tears.

Sources

For information about local happenings, check out the free English-language newspapers *Gringo Gazette* or *Destino: Los Cabos*. The English-Spanish *Los Cabos News* is also a good source for local events listings. These papers are available at most hotels and stores.

San José del Cabo

BARS

Local guides who work with kayaking and adventure-tourism companies hang out at **RAWHIDE** (Obregón at Guerrero, tel. 624/142–3626), an amiable cantina that's conducive to conversation. Two-for-one appetizers and happy-hour specials attract the early crowd, though the bar is open until 1 AM on Friday and Saturday, and until midnight during the week.

The 18-hole miniature golf course at the **RUSTY PUTTER** (Plaza Los Cabos, across from Fiesta Inn, tel. 624/142–4546), an open-air sports bar, is its best feature. Long holes, creative obstacles, and variations in the carpet make it a particularly good course. The bar and course are open 8 AM–1 AM.

TROPICANA BAR AND GRILL (Blvd. Mijares 30, tel. 624/142–1580) is an old standby where tourists mingle with locals. You can sit outside on the front patio or inside under the large *palapa* (palm thatch) roof. A small stage is set up for live music Friday and Saturday nights. Tropicana closes at 1 AM.

SHOOTERS SPORTS BAR (Manuel Doblado at Mijares, tel. 624/146–9900), on the rooftop at the Tulip Tree restaurant, shows sporting events on big screen TVs. It's open till everyone leaves.

LOS AMIGOS SMOKESHOP & CIGAR BAR (Hidalgo, tel. 624/142–1138) is the area's premier cigar shop. The bar hosts cigar tastings and Monday night football gatherings. You can sample from a wide selection of single malt scotch and fine tequilas.

JAZZ & SALSA
At the hip club **HAVANAS** (Hwy. 1, Km 29, no phone), owner Sheila Mihevic sings in an excellent jazz band that performs Wednesday through Friday. A six-piece salsa band delights locals and tourists of all ages on weekends. Though the crowd tends to be upscale, food and drink prices are reasonable. The open-air, second-level bar is filled with antiques from Cuba and some from an old saloon in Nevada. Havanas is closed Sunday and Monday.

MOVIES
At **CINEMA VERSAILLES** (Hwy. 1, Km 31, San José del Cabo, tel. 624/142–3333) admission is $3.50, but the selection of movies is generally three or four months behind what's showing in the

United States. Movies run in two theaters, with the last feature starting around 11 PM.

Cabo San Lucas

BARS

Quiet and refined **EL GALEÓN** (Blvd. Marina, tel. 624/143–0443) is just a few blocks from Cabo San Lucas's main strip, but this welcome refuge from the rowdy bars feels miles away. You don't have to dine at the Italian restaurant to sip brandy by the piano bar.

At the noisy, friendly **LATITUDE 22** (Av. Cárdenas, tel. 624/143–1516), the slogan is "No Bad Days." It's a long-standing place to down cold beers or shots of tequila and mingle with old and new friends. At this writing, owner Mike Grzanich is building an enormous restaurant–bar called the Roadhouse in the Corridor (Hwy. 1, Km. 4.5) and has put Latitude 22 up for sale. Check the status before heading out.

You can watch the action along the marina sidewalk from the **NOWHERE BAR** (Blvd. Marina 17 at Plaza Bonita, tel. 624/143–4493). There's usually a drink special and happy hour daily from 5 PM to 9 PM, plus good, inexpensive sushi. Dancing starts as the night goes on.

A hot spot for listening to live music, playing pool or darts, and watching sports on big-screen TVs, **TANGA TANGA** (Blvd. Marina outside the Plaza las Glorias Hotel, no phone) has a bar outdoors and another (air-conditioned) one inside. Local reggae and rock groups play here most afternoons and nights.

Sister location to the popular La Paz music club and bar, **LAS VARITAS** (Calle Gómez Farias by the fire station, tel. 624/143–9999) attracts locals in the know. One of Baja's top rock clubs, it hosts bands nearly every night.

Hagar's Hangout: Cabo Wabo

According to local lore, in the mid-1980s former Van Halen lead singer Sammy Hagar and a friend were walking along the beach in Cabo San Lucas when they passed a drunk man stumbling. Hagar remarked, "Hey, he's doing the Cabo Wabo." A few years later, in 1990, Hagar and the rest of Van Halen opened the bar called Cabo Wabo—establishing one of the premier stops on the Cabo party circuit. When the group broke up in 1996, all but Hagar sold their shares in the bar.

Mexican and American rock bands perform every night. Almost always packed, the place erupts when Hagar comes to play. When he's on tour, he may only make it to the club four or five times a year. Three of those visits fall on April 22 (the bar's anniversary), October 3–4 for the bar's MELT DOWN celebration, and October 7–13 (for Hagar's birthday celebration). When not on tour, Hagar hits Cabo Wabo up to 12 times a year. The dates are usually announced on the club's Web site, www. cabowabo.com.

Often accompanying Hagar are some of his rock-and-roll friends, who come to perform with him. These have included Chris Isaak, Kirk Hammett of Metallica, David Crosby, Slash, Rob Zombie, the Cult, and the Sex Pistols.

Easily seen from afar because of a lighthouse replica at the main entrance, the bar was designed by architect Marco Monroy. He built high, cavernous ceilings and painted the walls with zebra stripes and psychedelic neon patterns. Hagar liked Monroy's work so much that the design of the bar was replicated for his set on the "Red Voodoo" tour. The club has four pool tables and numerous bars, one hung with bras and panties donated over the years by female patrons.

BETTING

At **CALIENTE CASINO REAL** (Blvd. Marina at Plaza Nautica, tel. 624/143–1934), a gambling hall, restaurant, and bar, virtually any sporting event or horse race in the United States and Mexico is fair game. You can follow the results on one of more than 30 TVs. The bar, at the back of the smoky betting salon, is filled with red lounge chairs and black, fake marble tables. It's open 9 AM to midnight.

DANCE CLUBS

AGAIN & AGAIN (Av. Cárdenas between Leona Vicario and Morelos, tel. 624/143–6313) is the most attractive club in town. Two levels with pillared balconies overlook the stage and dance floor. On Thursday, the live *banda* (band) music draws a large crowd. The music, born in the 1950s in Monterrey, is traditional and often slow, for dancing in pairs. On other nights, the music is a mix of dance styles, including salsa and merengue.

One of the first establishments in town, the **GIGGLING MARLIN** (Blvd. Marina, tel. 624/143–1182) has retained its popularity over the years. Where else can you take a tequila shot while hanging upside down on a fish scale? The age of the clientele varies, as does the music, but the dance floor is usually jammed. A nightly two-for-one drinks special packs 'em in 11 PM to 1 AM. The bartender may place a shot of tequila in front of you the minute you sit down—you'll pay at least $5 if you drink it.

PAZZO'S (Morelos at Niños Heroes, tel. 624/143-4313) is a pizza joint gone wild, with bands playing from the second floor balcony overlooking the bar. Pasta dishes and pizzas provide the carbs to keep dancers moving late into the night. There's no official closing time.

If you have any religious sensitivity, moral convictions, or a heart condition, you may want to think twice before entering **SQUID ROE** (Av. Cárdenas, tel. 624/143–0655). Just about anything goes here: waiters dance and gyrate with female patrons, roaming waitresses shove Jell-O shots down your throat, frat-boy wannabes attempt beer-chugging contests, scantily clad dancers undulate in a makeshift penitentiary. During Spring Break or high season, more than 5,000 revelers come here on any given night—many stay until the 3 AM closing time.

GAY BARS

The main gay bar in San José del Cabo is **RAINBOW BAR** (Blvd. Marina at Marina Cabo Plaza, no phone). It's on the marina but away from the nightlife scene. The small, simple space has large mirrors on every wall, a tiny dance floor in the far corner, and two TVs that show music videos. It plays a good mix of English and Spanish music. The owner is American, but most of the patrons are Mexican men.

MOVIES

CINEMA PARAÍSO (Av. Cárdenas at Puerto Paraíso, tel. 624/143–1515) has four theaters, including a VIP screening room with reclining leather seats. First-run movies are shown in Spanish and English.

ROCK CLUBS

CABO WABO (Guerrero, tel. 624/143–1198), where "land ends and the party begins," has a rock band every night. But the impromptu jam sessions with appearances by former Van Halen singer Sammy Hagar—an owner—and his many music-business friends are the real highlight. There's a cover charge when Sammy and other big names are playing.

With its '59 pink Cadillac jutting through the window and dozens of rock-and-roll albums and other memorabilia on the walls, **HARD ROCK CAFE** (Blvd. Marina across from Squid Roe, tel. 624/143–7779) is a typical member of the chain. Live rock music starts at 10 every night. Thursday is ladies' night, when women drink free from 9 to 11.

A Shot of Tequila

What once was a drink of the poor Mexican farmer is now enjoyed by the international set and comes in nearly 1,000 varieties. Low-purity brands (like Cuervo Gold) that crowd shelves outside of Mexico have given tequila a reputation as a foul-tasting, noxious liquor. But aficionados compare a good tequila to fine cognac.

Tequila must contain at least 51% blue agave, a plant related to the lily. The best tequilas are 100% blue agave. Liquid is distilled from the sap of 7- to 10-year-old plants and fermented. Mezcal, a 100% blue agave cousin of tequila, is a liquor born in Oaxaca that is occasionally bottled with a worm (a practice that likely began as a marketing ploy). If you buy tequila with a worm, it was probably bottled in the United States, and is probably not good-quality tequila.

Most tequila is made in the town of Tequila, near Guadalajara. Labels bearing reposado indicate up to a year of aging; añejo, from one to three years. The longer tequila ages, the smoother it tastes. Sample a few before you buy; you're allowed only one liter through U.S. Customs.

WINE BARS

With 250 wines from all over the world, **SANCHO PANZA** (Blvd. Marina behind KFC and Plaza Las Glorias, tel. 624/143–3212) has the best wine list in town. Live blues or jazz fills the small bar every night. Though on the pricey side, the food is highly recommended. The bar closes at midnight and isn't open on Sunday.

She rolled out of bed and ambled to her luxurious marble bath. A steamy, soothing shower cleared her head, and not long after she'd wrapped herself in a thick terry robe came a knock on the door: breakfast. Was it enjoying the smoked-salmon omelet, table linens, and fresh flowers or dining on the balcony watching waves lap the shore that made her smile? It didn't matter. She was looking forward to another day with no clouds. Today she'd lounge by the fountain near the ocean-side pool before heading over to the spa.

In This Chapter

By Brad Weiss

Revised by Maribeth Mellin

where to stay

SPRAWLING MEXICAN- AND MEDITERRANEAN-STYLE RESORTS
dominate Los Cabos, especially along the Corridor. Hotel
developments have gobbled up most of San Lucas's waterfront,
and the amount of ongoing construction is astonishing. For years
building restrictions have been threatened—or promised,
depending on your view—but development continues.

Several megadevelopments in the Corridor contain two or more
hotels, along with golf courses and private villas, and guests
rarely leave the property. San José has large all-inclusive and time-
share properties along the beach. Some small hotels and bed-
and-breakfasts lie in or near town centers, and others are more
remote. Very few are beachfront, but great deals, friendly service,
and character make these inns popular. For high-season stays,
try to make reservations at least three months in advance, and six
months in advance for holidays. Precious few lodgings serve
travelers on a budget.

Note that time-share representatives at the airport and in many
hotel lobbies will try to entice you to attend a presentation by
offering free transportation, breakfast, or activities. Don't feel
obligated to accept—they often last at least two hours. If you're
staying in a hotel that has time-share units, aggressive
salespeople may call your room every morning asking you to
attend a free breakfast. If you're not interested, demand to be
taken off their call list.

PRICES

Bargains here are few and far between, and rooms at resort
hotels generally start at $200 a night. For groups of six or more

planning an extended stay, condos are a convenient and economical option. Otherwise, the best deals can be found at small bed-and-breakfasts, which are not plentiful and are usually booked early. You can find lower prices during off-season weeks—but don't expect huge discounts in Los Cabos.

We always list the facilities that are available, but we don't specify whether they cost extra; when pricing accommodations, always ask what's included and what costs extra.

Hotel rates in Baja California Sur are subject to a 10% value-added tax and a 2% hotel tax for tourism promotion. Service charges (at least 10%) and meals generally aren't included in hotel rates. Several of the high-end properties include a daily service charge in your bill; be sure you know the policy before tipping (though additional tips for extra service are always welcome). The Mexican government categorizes hotels, based on qualitative evaluations, into *gran turismo* (superdeluxe, or six-star, properties, of which there are only about 50 nationwide); five-star down to one-star; and economy class.

Assume that hotels operate on the European Plan (EP, with no meals) unless we specify that they offer a Continental Plan (CP, with a continental breakfast), Breakfast Plan (BP, with a full breakfast), Modified American Plan (MAP, with breakfast and dinner), or the Full American Plan (FAP, with all meals). Hotels in this guide have air-conditioning and private bathrooms with showers unless stated otherwise.

CATEGORY	COST*
$$$$	over $300
$$$	$200–$300
$$	$125–$200
$	$75–$125
¢	under $75

*All prices are for a standard double room, excluding service charges and 12% hotel occupancy tax.

Cabo Condos

If you're staying a week or more, renting a condo can be more economical and convenient than staying in a hotel. Los Cabos has countless condominium properties, from modest to ultraluxurious. Many private owners rent out their condos, either through the development's rental pool or property management companies. The price is the same, but with the latter you might get a better selection.

Nearly all condos are furnished and have a fully equipped kitchen, a television, bed and bath linens, laundry facilities, and maid service. Most are seaside and range from studios to three bedroom units. Though a minimum stay of one week is typically required, some condominiums require even longer stays. Start the process at least four months in advance, especially for high-season rentals. **CABO HOMES AND CONDOS** (tel. 624/142–6244, fax 624/142–6245, www.cabohomesandcondos.com) handles a large number of vacation rentals. **CABO VILLAS** (tel. 800/745–2226 in the U.S. and Canada, 831/475–4800 elsewhere, fax 831/475–4890, www.cabovillas.com) represents several properties including the high-end homes at Villas del Mar in the One&Only Palmilla compound.

SAN JOSÉ DEL CABO

$$$$ **PRESIDENTE INTER-CONTINENTAL LOS CABOS.** Set amid cactus gardens, this all-inclusive, family-welcoming hotel has three sections built around pools and lounging areas. The best rooms—with terraces—are on the ground floor. Note, though, that all rooms have showers instead of tubs. The rates include all meals, drinks, and some activities. You can choose between gourmet restaurants and themed buffets at dinner, order 24-hour room service, or opt for fast-food nachos, hot dogs, and fries at several food carts. Given the cost of eating out in Los Cabos and the quality of the food here, this is a good deal. As of this writing, the resort was also offering room-only rates of $130–$190, so ask if you'd prefer a noninclusive option. *Paseo San José at end of hotel zone, 23400, tel. 624/142–0211, 800/327–0200 in the U.S., fax 624/142–0232, loscabos.interconti.com. 395 rooms, 7 suites. 3 restaurants, room service,*

san josé del cabo lodging

TO LA PAZ AND AIRPORT

N

Ignacio Comonfort ⑦

⑨

Av. Zaragoza ⑥ ⑤

Av. Manuel Doblado ⑧

M. Castro ④

Coronado

Margarita Maza de Juárez ③

Cerro de la Cruz

Benito Juarez

Morelos

Miguel Hidalgo

① Valerio Gonzalez Canseco

Paseo de las Misiones

Cerro de El Vigia

Paseo Finisterra

Club de Golf

Blvd. Mijares

Carretera Transpeninsular

500 meters

500 yards

② Paseo Malecon San José

TO CABO SAN LUCAS

① Playa Hotelera

Golfo de California

Best Western Posada Real, 1	Posada Terranova, 8
Casa Natalia, 6	Presidente Inter-Continental Los Cabos, 2
El Encanto Hotel & Suites, 7	
La Fonda del Mar, 3	San José Youth Hostel, 9
Posada Señor Mañana, 5	Tropicana Inn, 4

in-room data ports, in-room safes, cable TV, 3 tennis courts, 3 pools, beach, fishing, horseback riding, shops, children's programs (ages 5–12), laundry service, business services, meeting rooms, car rental, travel services, no-smoking rooms. AE, MC, V. FAP.

$$$ ★ CASA NATALIA. Standing gracefully on San José's most charming street is this beautiful boutique hotel. The rooms are decorated in regional Mexican motifs and have king-size beds, remote-control air-conditioning, private patios, and cushy robes. The suites have hot tubs and hammocks on the large terraces. A complimentary shuttle takes guests to a beach club in the Corridor. The welcoming, personalized service is reinforced by the owners, who live on the premises. The restaurant, Mi Cocina, is worth seeking out. Children over 13 are welcome. Blvd. Mijares 4, 23400, tel. 624/142–5100, 888/277–3814 in the U.S., fax 624/142–5110, www.casanatalia.com. 14 rooms, 2 suites. Restaurant, room service, in-room data ports, in-room safes, pool, massage, bar, laundry service, concierge, airport shuttle. AE, MC, V. CP.

$$ BEST WESTERN POSADA REAL. One of the best values in the hotel zone, this beachside property consists of two trilevel, Santa Fe–style buildings. Every room has a balcony and at least a partial ocean view, a bathtub along with shower, and a refrigerator. The large heated pool has a palapa (palm thatch)-roof swim-up bar. The hotel is quiet compared to its all-inclusive neighbors and frequently draws business travelers. Malecón, hotel zone, 23400, tel. 624/142–0155, 800/528–1234 in the U.S., fax 624/142–0460, www.posadareal.com.mx. 140 rooms, 8 suites. 2 restaurants, room service, in-room data ports, in-room safes, cable TV, putting green, 2 tennis courts, pool, outdoor hot tub, beach, volleyball, 2 bars, shops, laundry service, Internet, meeting rooms, car rental. AE, MC, V.

$ EL ENCANTO HOTEL & SUITES. Near many of the town's best restaurants, this small European-style inn has two buildings—one with standard hotel rooms and a second across the street with suites. Both are surrounded by flower gardens with gurgling fountains; the suite building has a pool and patio where breakfast is served, as well as an art gallery. Rooms are immaculate; the largest suites (which run $125 per night) have kitchens and private patios. *Morelos 133, 23400, tel. 624/142–0388, fax 624/142–4620, www.elencantoinn.com. 12 rooms, 14 suites. Some kitchenettes, cable TV, pool, laundry service. AE, MC, V. CP.*

$ LA FONDA DEL MAR. If you're looking for peace and quiet, head for this out-of-the-way B&B that faces miles of secluded beach. It's home to the popular Buzzard's Bar & Grill, but it's otherwise blissfully tranquil at night (though trucks headed to construction sites in this rapidly growing area may rumble through during the day). Nevertheless, the three palm-thatch-roof cabañas and one suite are in heavy demand in high season. The whole operation runs on solar power; cabañas have en suite toilets and sinks but share a hot-water shower (the suite has private en suite facilities). To get here, turn off Boulevard Mijares at the signs for La Playa and follow the road up the hill past La Playa; it's about 10 minutes from San José. *Old East Cape Rd., 23400, tel. 702/255–0630 in the U.S., fax 624/142–1916, www.vivacabo.com. 3 cabañas, 1 suite. Restaurant, fans, beach, bar; no a/c. No credit cards. Closed part of August. BP.*

$ TROPICANA INN. If you aren't desperate to be on the beach, this small hotel in a quiet enclave behind San José's main boulevard is a great option. Stucco buildings with tile murals of Diego Rivera paintings frame a pool and a palapa bar. Rooms are maintained to look new and have cable TV. Book in advance in high season. *Blvd. Mijares 30, 23400, tel. 624/142–1580, fax 624/142–1590, www.tropicanacabo.com. 39 rooms, 2 suites, 1 house. Restaurant, room service, minibars, cable TV, pool, bar. AE, MC, V. CP.*

¢ POSADA SEÑOR MAÑANA. Accommodations at this quirky budget place run the gamut from small, no-frills rooms to larger quarters with air-conditioning, fans, cable TV, coffeemakers, and refrigerators. Hammocks hang on an upstairs deck, and you can store food and prepare meals in the communal kitchen. *Obregón by the Casa de la Cultura, 23400, tel. 624/142–0462, fax 624/142–1199,* *www.srmanana.net. 11 rooms. Fans, some refrigerators, pool; no a/c or TV in some rooms. MC, V.*

¢ **POSADA TERRANOVA.** San José's best inexpensive hotel is a friendly place where some guests return so frequently they're almost part of the family. The large rooms have two double beds and tile bathrooms. You can congregate at tables on the front patio or in the restaurant, and it still feels like a private home. *Calle Degollado at Av. Zaragoza, 23400, tel. 624/142–0534, fax 624/142–0902, www.hterranova.com.mx. 25 rooms. Restaurant, room service, cable TV, bar. AE, MC, V. CP.*

¢ **SAN JOSÉ YOUTH HOSTEL.** The rock-bottom conditions at this hostel don't discourage budget travelers who appreciate having a private bathroom for less than $10 per person for a double. Rooms vary from freshly painted to downright dreary; knowledge of Spanish helps when dealing with management and fellow guests. The market and the town's best taco stands are within easy walking distance. *Obregón, between Guerrero and Calle Degollado, 23400, tel. 044–624/355–3310 (cell phone). 20 rooms. Some fans; no a/c, no room phones, no room TVs. No credit cards.*

THE CORRIDOR

Even before the Corridor had an official name and a paved road, the hotels here were expensive and exclusive, with private airstrips. Little has changed, and developers have deliberately kept it high-end. It's the most valuable strip of real estate in the region, with golf courses, luxury developments, and unsurpassed views of the Sea of Cortez.

$$$$ **CASA DEL MAR GOLF RESORT AND SPA.** Luxurious privacy is the focus at Casa del Mar. The hotel has Saltillo (sun-dried clay tiles) tile floors, tile roofs, arched entryways, and carved wood furnishings. Rooms are designed to pamper—the bathrooms have whirlpool bathtubs and are set a few steps above the main bedroom, where cushy beds have satiny sheets and sea views.

118

the corridor lodging

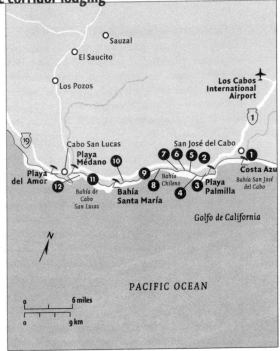

Cabo Surf Hotel, 1

Casa del Mar
Resort and Spa, 6

Casa
Terra Cotta, 2

Esperanza, 12

Hotel Cabo
San Lucas, 8

Marquis
Los Cabos, 5

Misiones
del Cabo, 11

One & Only
Palmilla, 3

Sheraton
Hacienda del Mar
Resort, 10

Twin Dolphin, 9

Las Ventanas
al Paraíso, 7

Westin Regina
Resort, 4

Guests in the suites receive complimentary Continental breakfast delivered to their rooms. The courtyard-lobby has stone fountains and stairways that curve up to the rooms. Flowing streams, fountains, and gardens lead around the pool to a wide stretch of untrammeled beach. *Hwy. 1, Km 19.5, Cabo San Lucas 23400, tel. 624/ 145–7700, 888/227–9621 in the U.S., fax 624/144–0034, www.casadelmarmexico.com. 25 rooms, 31 suites. 2 restaurants, room service, in-room data ports, in-room safes, in-room hot tubs, minibars, cable TV, golf privileges, 4 tennis courts, pool, gym, spa, sauna, steam room, beach, bar, library, shop, laundry service, concierge. AE, MC, V.*

$$$$ ESPERANZA. ★ The smallest suite at this lavish resort is 950 square feet. The suites, as well as several private villas, are decorated with original art, folk art, and handcrafted furnishings; some have private outdoor hot tubs. Frette linens, dual-head showers, plasma screen TVs, and DVD players in every suite or villa add to the extravagance. Some villas have hammocks and outdoor hot tubs. The spa has everything from warm springs and steam caves to exotic and traditional body treatments. At the restaurant, French and Mexican dishes are prepared with fresh seafood and organic produce. Rates start at $570 per night. *Hwy. 1, Km 3.5, Cabo San Lucas 23410, tel. 624/145–8641 or 866/311–2226 in the U.S., fax 624/ 145–8651, www.esperanzaresort.com. 50 suites, 6 villas. Restaurant, room service, in-room data ports, in-room safes, some kitchens, minibars, cable TV, pool, health club, outdoor hot tubs, spa, beach, snorkeling, windsurfing, boating, fishing, hiking, shops, laundry facilities, concierge, airport shuttle. AE, MC, V.*

$$$$ MARQUIS LOS CABOS. ★ Stunning architecture and attention to detail make the Marquis a worthy contender in the Corridor hotels' competition for wealthy clientele. The most-expensive casitas with private pools sit right on the beach, but even the standard suites are luxurious with Bulgari toiletries, reversible mattresses (hard or soft), high-speed Internet connections, and original art. The serpentine swimming pool curves along the edge of the sand, beneath waterfalls. The Mexican and international fare is excellent and reasonably priced. *Hwy. 1, Km 21.5, San José del Cabo 23410, tel. 624/144–0906, 877/238–9399 in the U.S., fax 624/144–0905, www.marquisloscabos.com. 209 suites, 28 casitas. 3 restaurants, room service, in-room data ports, in-room safes, in-room hot tubs, minibars, cable TV, golf privileges, pool, gym, spa, beach, bar, shop, concierge floor, Internet, business services, meeting rooms, airport shuttle, car rental, travel services, no-smoking rooms. AE, MC, V. CP.*

$$$$ ★ ONE&ONLY PALMILLA. Once a small, enchanting hotel, this property has been transformed into a world-class resort with contemporary rooms, a Mandara Spa, and a Charlie Trotter restaurant called C. Fortunately, designers retained the Spanish mission style, with its white arches and wedding chapel atop a hill. Tile stairways lead from flower-lined paths to luxurious rooms and suites with fabulous beds, deep bathtubs, and such high-tech amenities as Bose sound systems, flat-screen TVs, DVD players, and high-speed Internet access (with wireless in the works at press time). Some patios and terraces have daybeds loaded with pillows and straight-on views of the sea. Two pools seem to flow over low cliffs to the ocean. The golf course was designed by Jack Nicklaus. Room rates start at $475 per night; suites start at $1,100. *Hwy. 1, Km 7.5, San José del Cabo 23400, tel. 624/146–7000, 800/637–2226 in the U.S., fax 624/146–7001, www.oneandonlypalmilla.com. 61 rooms, 111 suites. 2 restaurants, room service, fans, in-room data ports, in-room safes, minibars, cable TV, 27-hole golf course, putting green, 2 tennis courts, pro shop, 2 pools, outdoor hot tub, fitness center, spa, beach, snorkeling, boating, 3 bars, shop, baby-sitting, laundry service, concierge, business services, meeting rooms, airport shuttle, car rental, travel services, no-smoking rooms. AE, MC, V.*

$$$$ SHERATON HACIENDA DEL MAR RESORT. Small tile domes painted red, orange, and pink top eight buildings at this majestic resort. Tasteful rooms are spacious and modern, and all have whirlpool tubs, original artwork, and large balconies with ocean views. The 450-yard beach below is beautiful to stroll, but strong currents make swimming dangerous. The location feels isolated and

Pamper Parlors

Los Cabos is nirvana for spa-lovers. Most spas in the high-end resorts are open to the public, and all offer massage treatments, from Swedish, deep-tissue, and sports to aromatherapy, shiatsu, and various forms of reflexology in the spa. Other high-demand services are body scrubs and wraps, in which sea salts, volcanic clay, seaweed, chamomile, or other natural elements exfoliate the skin and improve circulation. Cleansing, revitalizing facials are often used to treat wrinkles, acne, and sunburns.

Consistently rated one of the top spas in the world, **LAS VENTANAS AL PARAÍSO SPA** (Hwy. 1, Km 19.5, tel. 624/144–0300, www.lasventanas.com/spa.cfm) is a must for any spa addict. The rates for treatments are only slightly higher than at other area spas, yet the eclectic specialties range from ayurvedic body treatments and Indonesian traditional rituals, to ancient Tepezcohuite and Nopal (Mexican) healing wraps. **ESPERANZA** (Hwy. 1, Km 3.5, tel. 624/145–8641, www.esperanzaresort.com/spa.cfm) has a soothing full-service spa where guests are greeted with a choice of aguas frescas (fruit juices with water). To complete the pampering, waterfall showers and soaks in rock-enclosed hot tubs are available before and after treatments. Guests receive their treatments in private villas with hot tubs and sun beds at the Mandara Spa in the **ONE&ONLY PALMILLA** (Hwy. 1, Km 7.5, tel. 624/146–7000, www.oneandonlypalmilla.com). The spa at the **WESTIN REGINA GOLF & BEACH RESORT** (Hwy. 1, Km 22.5, tel. 624/142–9001, www.starwood.com/westin) is notable for its well-regarded therapists and its adjoining fitness center. Check out the reproductions of Baja's cave paintings at **VILLA DEL PALMAR SPA** (Old Road to San José, Km 0.5, tel. 624/143–4460). **PUEBLO BONITO ROSÉ SPA** (Playa Médano, tel. 624/143–5500, www.pueblobonito.com) is an elaborate affair with a Roman bath motif.

Spa packages combining three or four services can be relatively economical, although most still exceed $200. Nearly all spas also offer haircuts, manicures, pedicures, and waxing services. Many offer free use of fitness facilities—hot tub, steam room, sauna, and exercise equipment—with a spa treatment; otherwise, they may charge $15 to $25. No matter which spa you choose, make a reservation at least one day in advance.

luxurious. A $10 round-trip shuttle to Cabo San Lucas is a big plus. *Hwy. 1, Km 10, Cabo San Lucas 23410, tel. 624/145–8020, 888/672–7137 in the U.S., fax 624/145–8008, www.sheratonhaciendadelmar.com. 140 rooms, 31 suites. 4 restaurants, snack bar, room service, fans, in-room data ports, in-room safes, in-room hot tubs, some kitchens, minibars, cable TV, 4 pools, gym, hair salon, outdoor hot tub, spa, beach, 2 bars, shop, children's programs (ages 5–12), laundry service, Internet, business services, meeting rooms, car rental, travel services, no-smoking rooms. AE, DC, MC, V.*

$$$$ TWIN DOLPHIN Sleek and Japanese-modern, the Twin Dolphin has been a hideaway for the rich and famous since 1977 and has a loyal following of guests seeking seclusion. The minimalist rooms are in low-lying casitas along a seaside cliff. The hotel is worth a visit just to see the reproductions of Baja cave paintings on the lobby wall. Meal plans are available for an additional fee. *Hwy. 1, Km 11.5, Cabo San Lucas 23410, tel. 624/145–8190, 800/421–8925 in the U.S., fax 624/143–0496, 213/380–1302 in the U.S., www.twindolphin.com. 44 rooms, 6 suites. Restaurant, in-room safes, refrigerators, 2 tennis courts, pool, massage, beach, fishing, bar, shop, laundry service, no-smoking rooms; no room phones, no room TVs. MC, V.*

$$$$ LAS VENTANAS AL PARAÍSO. This hotel sets the standard for ★ luxury, privacy, and seaside elegance. Every suite has a wood-burning fireplace and a telescope for whale-watching and star-viewing. Sculpture, paintings, and handcrafted lamps and doors fill the place. Courteous staff seem to pop out of nowhere with a beach towel or a cool drink. Make reservations for both The Restaurant and the superb spa before your stay. At this writing, high-season rates ranged from $575 to $1,150 per night (with multiroom suites going up to $4,000). *Hwy. 1, Km 19.5, Cabo San Lucas 23400, tel. 624/144–0300, 888/767–3966 in the U.S., fax 624/144–0301, 310/824–1218 in the U.S., www.lasventanas.com. 61 suites. 3 restaurants, room service, in-room data ports, in-room safes, some in-room hot tubs, minibars, cable TV, in-room VCRs, golf privileges, 2 tennis courts, 2 pools, health club, hot tubs, spa, beach, snorkeling, windsurfing, boating, fishing, horseback riding, bar, shops, dry cleaning, laundry* service, meeting rooms, airport shuttle, travel services, some pets allowed (fee), no-smoking rooms. AE, MC, V.

$$$ HOTEL CABO SAN LUCAS. Looking like a mountain lodge nearly buried in palms, this long-standing Corridor hotel is a favorite of Baja devotees. Rooms are furnished with cheery yellow-and-blue fabrics and light-wood pieces; suites and villas are more luxurious with large terraces. The hacienda-style buildings are right above Chileno Beach, one of the best diving spots in Los Cabos. The excellent gift shop is worth a look even if you're not staying here. Hwy. 1, Km 14.5, Cabo San Lucas 23410, tel. 624/144–0014, 323/512–3799 or 866/733–2226 in the U.S., fax 624/144–0015, 323/512–3815 in the U.S., www.hotelcabo.com. 89 rooms, 7 villas. Restaurant, in-room safes, minibars, cable TV, pool, beach, dive shop, fishing, bar, shop, laundry service. AE, MC, V.

$$$ ★ WESTIN REGINA GOLF & BEACH RESORT. The architecturally astounding Westin is a magnificent conglomeration of colors, shapes, and views. The rooms, set above a man-made beach, are among the best in Los Cabos and have Westin's trademark heavenly beds with cushy pillows and comforters. Villas have full kitchens and whirlpool tubs that face the sea. Two of Los Cabos's best golf courses are nearby; otherwise, the hotel has so many amenities, including a fabulous spa and gym, you may never need to leave the grounds. It's a long walk from the parking lot and lobby to the rooms and pools, though. Hwy. 1, Km 22.5, Apdo. 145, San José del Cabo 23400, tel. 624/142–9001, 800/937–8461 in the U.S., fax 624/142–9010, www.starwood.com/westin. 243 rooms, 60 villas. 5 restaurants, room service, fans, in-room safes, some kitchens, kitchenettes, minibars, some refrigerators, cable TV with movies, 2 tennis courts, 7 pools, heath club, spa, outdoor hot tubs, beach, 4 bars, shops, children's programs (ages 5–12), babysitting, laundry service, concierge, business services, meeting rooms, travel services, no-smoking rooms. AE, MC, V.

$$–$$$ CABO SURF HOTEL. Legendary and amateur surfers alike claim the prime surf break-view rooms at this small hotel hidden in the cliffs above Playa Acapulquito and Costa Azul. They mingle by the horizon swimming pool and in the cozy restaurant and bar, and schedule their day's activities around the wave action. Rooms are spacious enough for two wave-hounds to spread out their gear; some have French doors that open to the sea breezes. Book early at this popular spot. *Hwy. 1 Km. 28, San José del Cabo 23410, tel. 624/142–2666, fax 624/142–2676, www.cabosurfhotel.com. 10 rooms. Restaurant, cable TV, some kitchenettes, pool, outdoor hot tub, bar. MC, V.*

$–$$ MISIONES DEL CABO. Some of the condos at this unpretentious complex have balconies with a hot tub and spectacular views of El Arco. Six beige Santa Fe–style buildings on a secluded beach house the condos, most of which have one or two bedrooms, though some are studios (the two-bedrooms run up to $315 per night). A free hotel shuttle runs back and forth to nearby San Lucas. Surfers enjoy the proximity to Monumentos, a great left break. *Hwy. 1, Km 5.5, Cabo San Lucas 23400, tel. 624/145–8090 or 800/524–5104, fax 624/145–8097. 42 condos. Restaurant, fans, kitchens, cable TV, in-room VCRs, 2 tennis courts, pool, outdoor hot tubs, shops, laundry service, no-smoking rooms. AE, MC, V.*

$ CASA TERRA COTTA. In the hills above Playa Costa Azul, this tiny bed-and-breakfast offers four secluded minivillas amid lush gardens. All have arched brick roofs, terra-cotta tile floors, and verandas ideal for whale-watching. The enormous breakfasts, made entirely with homegrown or organic ingredients, are legendary. Kitchen facilities are available to guests for a fee. Reserve at least six weeks in advance. *Hwy. 1, Km 28.5, ½ km [¼ mi] up hill, San José del Cabo 23410, tel. 624/142–4250, www.terracotta-mex.com. 4 suites. Dining room, massage, bar, laundry service; no in-room TVs. MC, V. BP.*

CABO SAN LUCAS

$$$ MARINA FIESTA. Though this colonial-style building is not ocean-side, most rooms have a pleasant view of the cloverleaf-shape pool and the yacht-filled marina just below. All rooms are spacious and handsome. The hotel is on the walkway around the marina, placing it about 500 yards from a number of bars and shops. Marina, lot 37, 23410, tel. 624/145–6020, fax 624/145–6021, www. marinafiestaresort.com. 139 rooms, 46 suites. Restaurant, grocery, room service, in-room safes, some in-room hot tubs, some kitchens, some kitchenettes, some minibars, cable TV, 2 pools, gym, outdoor hot tub, sauna, spa, bar, babysitting, playground, laundry service, Internet, business services, meeting rooms, travel services. AE, MC, V.

$$$ **MELIÁ SAN LUCAS.** The most popular beach in Los Cabos is where you'll find the Meliá and its huge, bustling pool areas, hot tub under the palms, and all the equipment you could need for playing on, and in, the water. Rooms have easygoing light-wood furnishings and heavy drapes to block out the midday sun. Early reservations are essential. Playa Médano, 23410, tel. 624/143–4444, 800/336–3542 in the U.S., fax 624/143–0418, www.solmelia.com. 144 rooms, 6 suites. 3 restaurants, in-room safes, minibars, cable TV, 2 pools, hot tub, beach, laundry service. AE, MC, V.

$$$ **PUEBLO BONITO ROSÉ.** Mediterranean-style buildings curve ☺ around the elegant grounds at this Playa Médano resort. Flemish tapestries decorate the spacious lobby, and statues recalling Roman busts guard reflecting pools. The spacious suites have private balconies overlooking the grounds; all have kitchenettes and even the smallest have plenty of room for four people. The spa facilities are open to the public for a fee. Many of the suites are used as time-share units, with guests booking in for a week. The time-share salespeople can be aggressive here, so make it clear from the start if you don't want to be bothered. Playa Médano, 23410, tel. 624/143–5500, 800/990–8250 in the U.S., fax 624/143–5979, www.pueblobonito.com. 260 suites. 2 restaurants, in-room safes, minibars, cable TV, pool, spa, beach, laundry service. MC, V.

$$$ **VILLA DEL PALMAR.** Both time-share and hotel guests appreciate ☺ the large rooms with kitchenettes and an array of amenities at this ever-growing property a 5-minute walk north of Playa Médano. The whale-shape waterslide at the three-level pool shows that families are welcome. The aroma of bread and pizzas baking in

cabo san lucas lodging

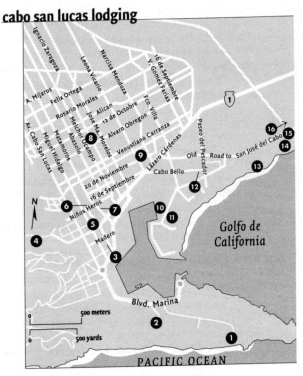

The Bungalows Breakfast Inn, 4

Cabo Inn, 9

Casa Bella, 5

Club Cabo Hotel, RV Park & Campground, 16

Finisterra, 2

Hotel Hacienda, 11

Hotel Melida, 6

Hotel Santa Fe, 8

Marina Fiesta, 10

Marina Sol Condominiums, 12

Los Milagros, 7

Meliá San Lucas, 13

Pueblo Bonito Rosé, 14

Siesta Suites, 3

Solmar Suites, 1

Villa del Palmar, 15

the wood-burning oven wafts from the first-rate open-air restaurant. Elegant condolike units are also available at the adjacent Villa la Estancia complex of private villas; rates for a one-bedroom villa start at $467. *Camino Viejo a San José, Km. 0.5, 23410, tel. 624/145–7000, fax 624/143–2664, www.villadelpalmarloscabos.com. 457 suites, 96 villas. 2 restaurants, room service, in-room data ports, in-room safes, some kitchens, kitchenettes, in-room VCRs, 2 pools, outdoor hot tubs, fitness center, spa, 2 bars, theater, shops, babysitting, children's programs (ages 4–12), laundry service, Internet, business services, meeting rooms, car rental. MC, V.*

$$–$$$ **HOTEL HACIENDA.** Sitting at the edge of the bay, the Hacienda resembles a Spanish colonial inn with white arches and bell towers, stone fountains, and statues of Indian gods set amid hibiscus and bougainvillea. The white rooms are decorated with red-tile floors, tile baths, and folk art. The water-sports center has any gear you might need. Though tiny, the Wellness Center offers excellent massages and holistic healing treatments, and the Cosmic Oyster Bar is a popular sunset-watching spot. *Playa Médano, 23410, tel. 624/143–0665, 624/143–0666, 800/733–2226 in the U.S., fax 624/143–0666, www.haciendacabo.com. 60 rooms, 12 suites, 30 beachfront cabañas. Restaurant, in-room safes, some kitchenettes, cable TV, pool, gym, massage, beach, bar, shops, laundry service. AE, MC, V.*

$$–$$$ **SOLMAR SUITES.** The Solmar sits against the cliffs at the tip of ★ Land's End, facing the Pacific. The rooms are decorated in Mexico–Santa Fe style, with tile baths. Adjacent time-share and condo units have kitchenettes and a private pool area. The surf here is far too dangerous for swimming, but don't miss a stroll along the wide strip of beach or a trip with the first-rate sportfishing fleet. The well-regarded restaurant hosts a Saturday-night Mexican fiesta and buffet dinner. *Av. Solmar at Blvd. Marina, Apdo. 8, 23410, tel. 624/143–3535, 310/459–9861 or 800/344–3349 in the U.S., fax 624/143–0410, 310/454–1686 in the U.S., www.solmar.com. 123 suites. Restaurant, in-room safes, some kitchenettes, minibars, cable TV, 3 pools, beach, fishing, bar, laundry service. AE, MC, V.*

$$ CASA BELLA. ★ The Ungson family had been in Cabo for more than four decades before turning their home across from Plaza San Lucas into a B&B. It's the classiest place in the neighborhood, landscaped with paths leading to a pool and terrace. The furnishings in the pretty rooms are handcrafted and thoughtfully arranged, and the huge hand-tiled bathrooms with open showers are works of art—some even have little gardens. The property feels totally secluded, though it's right in the middle of town. *Calle Hidalgo 10, 23410, tel. 624/143–6400, fax 624/143–6401, hotelboutiquecb@yahoo.com. 7 rooms, 1 suite. Pool, laundry service, no-smoking rooms; no room TVs. MC, V. CP.*

$$ FINISTERRA. One of the oldest hotels in Cabo, the Finisterra is also one of the most modern, with two towers that rise directly from the beach. An eight-story palapa covers the restaurant and bar on the beach next to two free-form swimming pools. Rooms in the new buildings are by far the nicest and have oceanfront balconies. The stone buildings of the less-expensive older section of the hotel evoke fishing lodges. The restaurant is good, and the Whale Watcher bar atop a high cliff has the best view in town. *Blvd. Marina, 23410, tel. 624/143–3333, 949/450–9000, 800/347–2252 in the U.S., fax 624/143–0590, 949/450–9010 in the U.S., www.finisterra.com. 287 rooms. 2 restaurants, some kitchenettes, minibars, cable TV, 2 tennis courts, 3 pools, sauna, spa, beach, 2 bars, babysitting, concierge, meeting rooms, car rental, travel services. AE, MC, V.*

$$ MARINA SOL CONDOMINIUMS. Good bargains can be found here—especially for groups of three to six people. Most of the condos are two-bedroom, but some have one, three, or five bedrooms. Only a few blocks from the town center and Playa Médano, this is a good spot if you like being close to the action. Reserve at least three months in advance for high season. Try to negotiate better rates for long-term stays. *Paseo del Pescador, 23410, tel. 624/143–3231 or 877/255–1721, fax 624/143–6286, www.marinasolresort.com. 36 condos. Restaurant, grocery, BBQs, fans, some kitchens, kitchenettes, microwaves, refrigerators, cable TV, some in-*

room VCRs, pool, gym, hair salon, outdoor hot tub, massage, bar, recreation room, shop, laundry service, Internet, business services. AE, MC, V.

$ THE BUNGALOWS BREAKFAST INN. If solitude and a reasonable room rate are more important than being in the center of things, this is your place. In several two-story buildings that frame a small, heated pool, the rooms are smartly decorated with Mexican textiles and art. It's located about 10 blocks from the beach. *Calle Constitución, 5 blocks from main plaza, 23410, tel. 888/424–2252 in the U.S., tel./fax 624/143–5035, www.cabobungalows.com. 16 suites. Some kitchenettes, cable TV, in-room VCRs, pool; no smoking. No credit cards. BP.*

¢ CABO INN. What this small palapa-roof hotel lacks in luxury, it makes up for in character. The small, comfortable rooms have tangerine and cobalt sponge-painted walls and stained-glass windows above the headboards. The eight rooms on the lower level have refrigerators; a kitchen, barbecue and picnic area, and a television round out the communal amenities. *Calle 20 de Noviembre and Vicario, 23410, tel./fax 624/143–0819. 21 rooms. Picnic area, refrigerators; no room TVs. No credit cards.*

¢ CLUB CABO HOTEL, RV PARK & CAMPGROUND. Though only a five-minute drive from Playa Médano, this small complex is quiet and remote. It sits amid dense vegetation between the beach and Highway 1 and has tent and RV camping alongside well-maintained motel rooms and a long pool. Parking is secure and prices very reasonable. Reservations are accepted for rooms but not for the RV/tent sites. *Off Old Road to San José, Km 3, just east of Villa del Palmar, 23410, tel./fax 624/143–3348, www.mexonline. com/clubcabo.htm. 10 rooms, 18 tent/RV sites. Fans, some kitchenettes, some refrigerators, TV, pool, laundry facilities, Internet. No credit cards.*

¢ HOTEL MELIDA. This bare-bones hotel in a commercial neighborhood offers simple but immaculately clean rooms. The televisions are encased in metal cages, which makes one wonder about the clientele. But the management is friendly and helpful, and you can walk to Playa Médano in about 15 minutes. It's just a few blocks away from the bars by the marina, which may explain the precautions. Noise can be a problem. *Matamoros at Niños Héroes, 23410, tel. 624/143–6564. 14 rooms. Shop. No credit cards.*

¢ HOTEL SANTA FE. There's a friendly, make-yourself-at-home feeling at this small hotel that resembles a two-story apartment building. Room service is provided by the deli at the adjacent market. Large rooms have sofa beds and cable TV. The beach is a 10-minute walk away and the pool isn't heated. Ask about deals for weekly stays. *Av. Zaragoza and Obregón, 23410, tel. 624/143–4401, fax 624/143–4402. 46 rooms. Grocery, room service, fans, kitchenettes, pool, laundry facilities, laundry service. MC, V.*

¢ LOS MILAGROS. A mosaic sign (made by co-owner Ricardo Rode) ★ near the entrance hints at the beauty inside this small inn in the town center. Brilliant purple bougainvillea and orange lipstick vines line the patio, which showcases more of Rode's works by the fountain and small pool. Arched boveda-style roofs top the rooms, which have terra-cotta tile floors and handmade Guadalajaran furniture. Guests gather with co-owner Sandra Scandiber at the patio table and on a peaceful sundeck to share budget travel tips. One room is accessible to travelers with disabilities. Book early at this Cabo bargain. *Matamoros 116, 23410, tel. 718/928–6647 in the U.S., tel./fax 624/143–4566, www.losmilagros.com.mx. 11 rooms. Some kitchenettes, cable TV, pool, library, laundry service, Internet, business services. No credit cards.*

¢ SIESTA SUITES. This oasis of calm off the main drag offers a lot for the money. There's no pool, but the suites have full-size refrigerators, and between the two double beds and the wide padded couches that make excellent beds even for grown-ups, you'll have room to sleep quite a crew. The three-story hotel sits two blocks from the marina. The proprietors keep a close eye on the place and offer great budget tips. A small restaurant and wine bar beside the hotel serves tapas and full dinners. *Calle Zapata, Apdo. 310, 23410, tel./fax 624/143–6494, 866/271–0952 in the*

U.S., *www.cabosiestasuites.com.* 5 rooms, 15 suites. Kitchenettes, cable TV. AE, MC, V.

BEYOND LOS CABOS

East Cape

$$ HOTEL BUENA VISTA BEACH RESORT. Tile-roof bungalows sit along flower-lined paths next to pools, fountains, and lawns at this low-key hotel. All rooms have tile floors and light floral drapes and spreads; some have private terraces. Those in the older section near the entrance are more private, while the newer rooms by the pool are good for families with kids who want to splash all day. The fishing fleet is excellent, as are other diversions, such as diving, snorkeling, kayaking, horseback riding, and trips to natural springs. A European plan without meals is available from November through March, which cuts the rate in half. *Hwy. 1, Km 105, Buena Vista 23500, tel. 624/141–0033, 619/429–8079, 800/ 752–3555 in the U.S., fax 624/141–0133, www.hotelbuenavista.com. 60 rooms. Restaurant, tennis court, 2 pools, hot tub, massage, beach, fishing, horseback riding, meeting rooms, car rental; no room TVs, no room phones. MC, V. FAP.*

$$ HOTEL PALMAS DE CORTEZ. Often featured on sportfishing shows, this hotel is near the famed Cortez banks and has its own fleet. It has evolved into a full-blown resort and social center for the East Cape. Special events, including an annual festival of the arts in March, attract local crowds. Its enormous swimming pool has a swim-up bar. White walls, archways, terra-cotta floors and painted-tile bathrooms give the rooms a Mexican flair; some have stone fireplaces and/or full kitchens. The same company runs two other hotels in the area. *On the beach; take the road north through Los Barriles and continue to the beach, Los Barriles (Box 9016 Calabasas, CA 91372), tel. 624/141–0214, 800/368–4334 in the U.S., fax 624/141– 0046, www.bajaresorts.com. 20 rooms, 15 suites, 10 condos. Restaurant, some kitchens, tennis court, pool, gym, fishing, playground, Internet, airstrip, meeting rooms. MC, V. FAP.*

La Paz

$ EL ÁNGEL AZUL. Owner Esther Ammann converted the city's
★ historic courthouse into a charming bed-and-breakfast whose
rooms frame a central courtyard and are decorated with original
artwork. The rooftop suite (the only unit with a TV) overlooks the
city. *Av. Independencia 518, at Guillermo Prieto, 23000, tel. 612/125–
5130, www.elangelazul.com. 10 rooms, 1 suite. Bar, no-smoking rooms;
no room TVs, no kids under 12. MC, V. CP.*

$ LA CONCHA BEACH RESORT. The only full-scale resort on the
beach in La Paz, La Concha has a long beach with calm water, a
complete water-sports center, and a notably good restaurant.
Unfortunately, the standard rooms can be dark and uninviting,
so you may want to splurge on a cheerier condo unit with a
separate bedroom and kitchen; the smallest run around $135 per
night. There's a shuttle to town. *Carretera a Pichilingue, Km 5,
between downtown and Pichilingue, 23010, tel. 612/121–6344, 612/121–
6161, 800/999–2252 in the U.S., fax 612/121–6218, www.laconcha.com.
107 rooms. Restaurant, minibars, cable TV, pool, beach, dive shop, 3
bars, laundry service, shops, car rental, travel services. AE, MC, V.*

Todos Santos

$$ POSADA LA POZA. Looking for a civilized, self-contained retreat?
The Swiss owners here aim to please with their chic posada beside
a bird-filled lagoon and the open sea. The suites are handsomely
decorated with rust-tone walls, modern furniture, and Swiss
linens; you'll have a CD player and binoculars on hand, but no
TVs or phones to distract you. There's a palm-fringed pool and a
terrific restaurant—even if you're not staying, come by for
fettuccine with white truffle sauce and organic salads. The
restaurant is closed Thursday. *Follow the signs on Hwy. 19 and on
Av. Juárez to the beach, 23305, tel. 612/145–0400, fax 612/145–0453,
www.lapoza.com. 7 rooms. Restaurant, in-room safes, minibars, pool,
massage, bar, Internet; no room phones, no room TVs. MC, V. BP.*

$–$$ TODOS SANTOS INN. The six guest rooms in this converted 19th-century house are unparalleled in design and comfort. Gorgeous antiques are set against stone walls under brick ceilings. Ceiling fans and the shade from garden trees keep the rooms cool and breezy. The inn's wine bar is open in the evening, and good restaurants are within easy walking distance. *Calle Legaspi, 23305, tel./fax 612/145–0040, www.todossantosinn.com. 6 rooms. Bar; no a/c in some rooms, no room phones, no room TVs. No credit cards.*

$ HOTEL CALIFORNIA. New owners transformed this hotel with a famous name from a run-down shell to a sophisticated inn. The previous proprietors encouraged the rumor that the Eagles' song originated here, but now that the myth has been debunked, this handsome place should draw guests on its own merits. A deep blue-and-ochre color scheme runs throughout, and the rooms are furnished with an eclectic mix of antiques and folk art. Some rooms have ocean views; at this writing, five additional rooms are being added. The bar has become a local hot spot. *Calle Juárez at Morelos, 23305, tel. 612/145–0525, fax 612/145–0288. 6 rooms. Restaurant, pool, bar; no a/c, no room TVs, no room phones. MC, V.*

practical information

Addresses

Many addresses in Mexico have "s/n" for *sin número* (no number) after the street name. This is common throughout Mexico, as is the practice of listing cross streets in an address. Similarly, many Cabo hotels give their address as "Carretera Cabo San Lucas–San José del Cabo, Km 19" which indicates that the property is at the 19th kilometer on the *carretera* (main highway) between Cabo San Lucas and San José del Cabo. Some properties in the Corridor call the highway the "Corredor Turistico" or the "Carretera Transpeninsular," although this book refers to this road as Highway 1.

Other abbreviations used in addresses include the following: Av. (*avenida*, or avenue), Calz. (*calzada*, or road), Fracc. (*fraccionamiento*, or housing estate), and Int. (interior).

Addresses in Mexico are written with the street name first, followed by the street number. A five-digit *código postal* (C.P.; postal code) precedes, rather than follows, the name of the city. Apdo. (*apartado*) is short for box; Apdo. Postal, or A.P., means post-office box number.

Air Travel

BOOKING

When you book, look for nonstop flights and remember that "direct" flights stop at least once. Try to avoid connecting flights, which require a change of plane. Two airlines may operate a connecting flight jointly, so ask whether your airline operates every segment of the trip; you may find that the carrier you prefer flies you only part of the way. To find more booking tips and to check prices and make online flight reservations, log on to www.fodors.com.

CARRIERS

Aeroméxico flies nonstop to Los Cabos (San José del Cabo) from SanDiego. American flies nonstop from Dallas/Fort Worth, Chicago, and Los Angeles; Delta flies from Atlanta; Continental flies nonstop from Houston; AeroCalifornia flies nonstop from Los Angeles; Mexicana flies from Los Angeles and Denver; Alaska Airlines flies nonstop from Los Angeles, San Diego, Phoenix, San Jose, San Antonio, and San Francisco; America West flies nonstop from Phoenix. Some airlines may offer nonstop flights from other U.S. cities during the winter season.

European airlines fly to Mexico City, where connections can be made for the two-hour flight to Los Cabos. Air France offers service from Paris; British Airways from London; Iberia from Madrid; and Lufthansa from Frankfurt. Keep in mind that schedules and airlines change constantly.

➤AIRLINES & CONTACTS: AeroCalifornia (tel. 800/237–6225, 624/143–3700 in Los Cabos). Aeroméxico (tel. 800/237–6639, 624/142–0398 in Los Cabos). Air France (tel. 800/237–2747). Alaska Airlines (tel. 800/426–0333, 01–800/252–7522 in Mexico, 624/146–5097 in Los Cabos). American (tel. 800/433–7300, 01–800/906–6000 in Mexico, 624/146–5304 in Los Cabos). America West (tel. 800/235–9292, 624/142–2362 in Los Cabos). British Airways (tel. 800/247–9297, 5525/387–0300 in Mexico City). Continental (tel. 800/523–3273, 01–800/523–3273 in Mexico). Delta (tel. 800/241–4141). Iberia (tel. 020/7830–0011). Lufthansa (tel. 0181/750–3535). Mexicana (tel. 800/531–7921, 01–800/719–1956 in Mexico, 624/142–0230 in Los Cabos).

CHECK-IN & BOARDING

Always find out your carrier's check-in policy. Plan to arrive at the airport about two hours before your scheduled departure time for domestic flights and 2½ to 3 hours before international flights. You may need to arrive earlier if you're flying from one of the busier airports or during peak air-traffic times.

Assuming that not everyone with a ticket will show up, airlines routinely overbook planes. When everyone does, airlines ask for volunteers to give up their seats. In return, these volunteers usually get a several-hundred-dollar flight voucher, which can be used toward the purchase of another ticket, and are rebooked on the next flight out. If there are not enough volunteers, the airline must choose who will be denied boarding. The first to get bumped are passengers who checked in late and those flying on discounted tickets, so get to the gate and check in as early as possible, especially during peak periods.

Always **bring a government-issued photo ID** to the airport; even when it's not required, a passport is best.

FLYING TIMES

Via nonstop service, Los Cabos is about 2 hours from San Diego, about 2¼ hours from Houston, 3 hours from Dallas/Fort Worth, 2½ hours from Los Angeles, and 2½ hours from Phoenix. Flying time from New York to Mexico City, where you must switch planes to continue to Los Cabos, is 5 hours. Los Cabos is about a 2 ½-hour flight from Mexico City, where flights from Europe connect.

RECONFIRMING

Check the status of your flight before you leave for the airport. You can do this on your carrier's Web site, by linking to a flight-status checker (many Web booking services offer these), or by calling your carrier or travel agent. Always confirm international flights at least 72 hours ahead of the scheduled departure time.

Airports & Transfers

AIRPORTS

Aeropuerto Internacional Los Cabos (SJD) is 1 km (½ mi) west of the Transpeninsular Highway (Hwy. 1), 13 km (8 mi) north of San José del Cabo, and 48 km (30 mi) northeast of Cabo San Lucas. The airport has restaurants, duty-free shops, and car-rental agencies. Alaska Airlines has a separate terminal with all services at the airport.

Aeropuerto General Manuel Márquez de León serves La Paz. It's 11 km (7 mi) northwest of the Baja California Sur capital, which itself is 188 km (117 mi) northwest of Los Cabos.

➤AIRPORT INFORMATION: Aeropuerto General Manuel Márquez de León (tel. 612/112–0082). Aeropuerto Internacional Los Cabos (tel. 624/146–5013).

TRANSFERS

If you have purchased a vacation package from an airline or travel agency, transfers are usually included. Otherwise, only the most exclusive hotels in Los Cabos offer transfers. Shuttle buses drop passengers off at all hotels for $15–$25 a person; this is the least expensive way to go but is not recommended for anyone in a hurry. Some hotels can arrange a pickup, which is much faster and might cost about the same as a shuttle. Ask about the fare when making your reservation. Take advantage of hotel transfers if you're staying in the East Cape, La Paz, and Todos Santos, and you're not renting a car—cab fares to these areas are astronomical.

Unless you want to tour a time-share or real estate property, ignore the offers for free transfers when you come out of customs. The scene can be bewildering for first timers. Sales representatives from various time-share properties compete vociferously for clients; often you won't realize you've been suckered into a time-share presentation until you get in the van. To avoid this situation, go to the official taxi booths inside the baggage claim or just outside the final customs clearance area and pay for a ticket for a regular shuttle bus. Private taxis, often U.S. vans, are expensive and not metered, so **always ask the fare before getting in.** Rates change frequently, but for one to four persons, it costs about $15 to get to San José del Cabo, $26 to a hotel along the Corridor, and $50 to Cabo San Lucas. After the fourth passenger, it's about an additional $3 per person. Usually only vans accept more than four passengers. At the end of your trip, **don't wait until the last minute to book return transport.** Make arrangements a few days in advance for shuttle service, or sign up at your hotel to share a cab with other travelers.

Boat Travel

Ferry service runs from Mazatlán and Topolobampo on mainland Mexico to La Paz. Some ferries carry vehicles as well as passengers.

FARES & SCHEDULES

Sematur operates the ferries between La Paz and Mazatlán. Schedules and fares are available by phone or on the Sematur Web site, but bookings must be made at the Sematur offices. Baja Ferries offers daily service between La Paz and Topolobampo. Round-trip fare is $58; add $72 if you book a cabin.

▶BOAT INFORMATION: **Baja Ferries** (tel. 800/884–3107, www.nativetrails.com/Baja-Ferry/ferry.htm). **Sematur** (Calle 5 de Mayo 502, La Paz, tel. 612/125–2366, 01–800/696–9600 in Mexico; Prolongación Carnaval s/n, Mazatlán, tel. 669/981–7020, www.sematur.com.mx).

Bus Travel

First-class buses are punctual and comfortable, with restrooms and assigned seats. On overnight bus rides, **bring something to** eat (bus-stop restaurants can be unappealing or unsanitary) and carry toilet tissue, as restrooms might not have any.

Bus service to Los Cabos from Tijuana is not recommended unless you have plenty of time or plan to stop along the way. The entire trip takes about 22 hours and costs about $94 one-way. In Tijuana, buses leave from the Central de Autobuses. Greyhound buses from the United States make connections at the Tijuana terminal with the company's subsidiary, Greyhound de México. (Call the office in San Diego for the most accurate information.) Mexican lines include Autotransportes de Baja California (ABC).

Águila has the most comfortable bus trips to Todos Santos or La Paz from Los Cabos. The buses have air-conditioning and restrooms. Buses usually leave every hour (always check to be sure) from both the San José and Cabo San Lucas terminals. One-way fare is $4 (payable in pesos or dollars) to Todos Santos and $10 to La Paz. From the Corridor, expect to pay about $25 for a taxi to the bus station.

The trip between San José del Cabo and Cabo San Lucas takes about 35 minutes by bus. Trans Cabo buses run along the Corridor between the two towns, with stops along the way. The bus runs every half-hour from 7 AM to 10 PM; the fare is about $2. Autotransportes El Águila buses usually run every half hour from 5:45 AM to 8 PM between the bus stations in the two towns. There are no stops along the Corridor, but drivers might drop you off by your hotel if you ask. Fare is about $3.

➤BUS INFORMATION: **Autotransportes El Águila** (tel. 612/122–4270). **Autotransportes de Baja California** (ABC) tel. 664/621–3038 in Tijuana, 612/122–6476 in La Paz). **Cabo San Lucas Bus Terminal** (5 de Febrero, at Carretera Todos Santos, tel. 624/143–7878). **Central de Autobuses** (Calzada Lázaro Cárdenas and Arroyo Alamar, Tijuana, tel. 664/621–2982). **Greyhound de México** (tel. 800/231–2222, 664/621–1948 in Tijuana, 619/239–3266 in San Diego). **San José del Cabo**

Bus Terminal (Valerio González, Colonia 1 de Mayo, on the southwest edge of town near Hwy. 1, tel. 624/142–1100). **Trans Cabo** (tel. 624/146–0888).

PAYING

All bus tickets can be purchased on the spot, except during holidays, when an advance purchase is crucial. Payment can be in pesos or U.S. dollars, although some of the deluxe bus services accept major credit cards such as Visa and MasterCard.

Business Hours

Banks are usually open weekdays 8:30 AM–3 PM. Government offices are usually open to the public weekdays 8–3; they are closed—along with banks and most private offices—on national holidays. Stores are generally open weekdays and Saturday from 9 or 10 AM to 7 or 8 PM. In tourist areas, some shops don't close until 10 PM and are open Sunday. Some shops close for a two-hour lunch break, usually from 2 to 4. Shops extend their hours when cruise ships are in town.

Car Rental

Taxi fares are steep, and a car can come in handy if you plan to dine at the Corridor hotels or travel frequently between the two towns, or if you're spending more than a few days in Los Cabos. If you don't want to rent a car, your hotel concierge or tour operator can arrange for a car with a driver or limousine service.

Convertibles and jeeps are popular rentals, but beware of sunburn and windburn and remember there's nowhere to stash your belongings out of sight. Specify whether you want air-conditioning and manual or automatic transmission. A VW convertible with manual transmission rents for about $80 a day or $560 a week; a Jeep Wrangler goes for about $120 a day, and $840 a week. Rates include unlimited mileage, 10% tax, and insurance. Rates for air-conditioned, automatic-transmission compacts or subcompacts range from $95 to $120 a day, while wagons and heavy-duty vehicles go for about $150 to $180 a day, including tax and insurance. Most vendors negotiate considerably if tourism is slow; ask about special rates if you're renting by the week.

To increase the likelihood of getting the car you want, **make arrangements before you leave for your trip.** Also, call around, because rates can vary widely. You can sometimes, but not always, find cheaper rates on the Internet, but no matter how you book, rates are generally much lower when you reserve a car in advance outside of Mexico.

➤**AGENCIES: Advantage** (tel. 800/777–5500, 020/8897–0811 in the U.K., www.advantagerentacar.com). **Alamo** (tel. 800/ 522–9696, www.alamo.com). **Avis** (tel. 800/331–1084, 800/ 879–2847 in Canada, 0870/606–0100 in the U.K., 02/9353– 9000 in Australia, 09/526–2847 in New Zealand, www. avis.com). **Budget** (tel. 800/527–0700, 0870/156–5656 in the U.K., www.budget.com). **California Baja Rent-A-Car** (tel. 619/ 470–8368 or 888/470–7368, www.cabaja.com). **Dollar** (tel. 800/800–6000, 0800/085–4578 in the U.K., www.dollar.com). **Hertz** (tel. 800/654–3001, 800/263–0600 in Canada, 0870/ 844–8844 in the U.K., 02/9669–2444 in Australia, 09/ 256–8690 in New Zealand, www.hertz.com). **National Car Rental** (tel. 800/227–7368, 0870/600–6666 in the U.K., www. nationalcar.com).

INSURANCE

In Mexico you must have Mexican auto insurance, which can be purchased at the rental agency. Full coverage is about $19–$25 a day.

REQUIREMENTS & RESTRICTIONS

In Mexico your own driver's license is acceptable. A universally recognized International Driver's Permit can save you from hassles with local authorities. It's available from the U.S.

and Canadian automobile associations, and, in the United Kingdom, from the Automobile Association or Royal Automobile Club.

In most cases, the minimum rental age is 25, although some companies will lower it to 22 for an extra daily charge. A valid driver's license, major credit card, and Mexican car insurance are required.

Car Travel

There are two absolutely essential points to remember about driving in Mexico. First and foremost is to **carry Mexican auto insurance.**

Secondly, **if you enter Mexico with a car, you must leave with it.** In recent years, the high rate of U.S. vehicles being sold illegally in Mexico has caused the Mexican government to enact stringent regulations for bringing a car into the country—at great inconvenience to motoring American tourists. If an emergency arises and you must fly home, there are complicated customs procedures to face.

You must **bring the following documents in order to drive into Mexico:** title or registration for your vehicle; a birth certificate or passport; a credit card (AE, DC, MC, or V); and a valid driver's license with a photo. The title holder, driver, and credit-card owner must be one and the same—if your spouse's name is on the title of the car and yours isn't, you cannot bring the car into the country without your spouse. For financed, leased, rental, or company cars, you must **bring a notarized letter of permission** from the bank, lien holder, rental agency, or company.

When you submit your paperwork at the border, your credit card is charged $12 and you receive a tourist visa, a car permit, and a sticker to put on your vehicle, all valid for up to six months. Be sure to **turn in the permit and the sticker at the border** prior to their expiration date; otherwise you could incur high fines. The person whose name is on the paperwork must be the person who returns the car. A time-saving alternative is to **have your paperwork done in advance** at a branch of Sanborn's Mexican Insurance; look in the Yellow Pages for an office in almost every town on the U.S.–Mexico border. There is a $10 charge for this service.

EMERGENCIES

The Mexican Tourism Ministry operates a fleet of more than 350 pickup trucks, known as the Angeles Verdes, or Green Angels. Bilingual drivers provide mechanical help, first aid, radio-telephone communication, basic supplies and small parts, towing, tourist information, and protection. Services are free; spare parts, fuel, and lubricants are provided at cost. Tips are always appreciated ($5–$10 for big jobs, $2–$3 for minor repairs). The Green Angels patrol sections of the major highways daily 8 AM–8 PM (later on holiday weekends). If you break down, **pull off the road as far as possible,** lift the hood of your car, hail a passing vehicle, and ask the driver to **notify the patrol.** Most bus and truck drivers will be quite helpful. If you witness an accident, do not stop to help—it could be a ploy to rob you or could get you interminably involved with the police. Instead, notify the nearest official.

➤**CONTACTS: Green Angels, La Paz** (tel. 612/125–9677).

GASOLINE

Pemex (the government petroleum monopoly) franchises all gas stations in Mexico. Stations are located on the outskirts of San José del Cabo and Cabo San Lucas and in the Corridor. Gas is measured in liters. Gas stations in Los Cabos may not accept credit cards. Prices run higher than in the United States. Premium unleaded gas (*magna premio*) and regular unleaded gas (*magna sin*) is available nationwide, but it's still a good idea to **fill up whenever you can.** Fuel quality is generally lower than that in the United States and Europe. Vehicles with fuel-injected engines are likely to have problems after driving extended distances.

Gas-station attendants pump the gas for you and may also wash your windshield and check your oil and tire air pressure. A tip of 5 or 10 pesos (about 50¢ or $1) is customary depending on the number of services rendered, beyond pumping gas.

INSURANCE

You must **carry Mexican auto insurance**, which you can purchase near border crossings on either the U.S. or Mexican side. If you injure anyone in an accident, you could well be jailed—whether it was your fault or not—unless you have insurance. It is difficult to arrange bail once you are jailed, and it can take months for your case to be heard by the courts. Purchase enough Mexican automobile insurance at the border to cover your estimated trip. It's sold by the day, and if your trip is shorter than your original estimate, some companies might issue a prorated refund for the unused time upon application after you exit the country. If you're an AAA (American Automobile Association) member, you can purchase Mexican insurance in advance; call your local AAA office for details.

➤**CONTACTS: American Automobile Association** (www.aaa.com). **Instant Mexico Auto Insurance** (223 Vía de San Ysidro, San Ysidro, CA 92173, tel. 619/428–3583). **Oscar Padilla** (4330 La Jolla Village Dr., San Diego, CA 92122, tel. 800/258–8600). **Sanborn's Mexican Insurance** (2009 S. 10th St., McAllen, TX 78503, tel. 210/686–0711 or 800/222–0158).

ROAD CONDITIONS

Mexico Highway 1, also known as the Carretera Transpeninsular, runs the entire 1,700 km (1,054 mi) from Tijuana to Cabo San Lucas. Occasional bad weather and repairs can make for slow going. Do not drive the highway at high speeds or at night—it is not lighted.

Highway 19 runs between Cabo San Lucas and Todos Santos, joining Highway 1 below La Paz. The four-lane road between San José del Cabo and Cabo San Lucas is usually in good condition, although dips and bridges become flooded in heavy rains and sections are frequently destroyed by hurricanes. Roadwork along the highway is common.

In rural areas, roads are quite poor. **Use caution, especially during the rainy season,** when rock slides and potholes are a problem, and **be alert for animals**—cattle, coyotes, and dogs in particular—especially on the highways. If you have a long distance to cover, **start early and fill up on gas**; don't let your tank get below half full. Allow extra time for unforeseen obstacles.

Signage is not always adequate in Mexico, and the best advice is to **travel with a companion and a good map.** Always lock your car, and never leave valuable items in the body of the car (the trunk will suffice for daytime outings, but don't pack it in front of prying eyes).

The Mexican Tourism Ministry distributes free road maps from its tourism offices outside the country. Guía Roji and Pemex publish current city, regional, and national road maps, which are available in bookstores and big supermarket chains for under $10; gas stations generally do not carry maps.

RULES OF THE ROAD
When you sign up for Mexican car insurance, you should receive a booklet on Mexican rules of the road. Read it.

Illegally parked cars are either towed or have wheel blocks placed on the tires, which can require a trip to the traffic-police headquarters for payment of a fine. It is almost always safer to **park in a lot instead of on the street.**

If an oncoming vehicle blinks its lights at you in the daytime, slow down: it could mean trouble ahead. When approaching a narrow bridge, the first vehicle to flash its lights has the right of way. One-way streets are common. One-way traffic is indicated by an arrow; two-way, by a double-pointed arrow. A circle with a diagonal line superimposed on the letter E (for *estacionamiento*) means "no parking." Other road signs follow the now widespread system of international symbols, a copy of which will usually be provided when you rent a car in Mexico.

Mileage and speed limits are given in kilometers: 100 kph and 80 kph (62 and 50 mph, respectively) are the most common maximums. A few of the newer toll roads allow 110 kph (68 mph). In cities and small towns, **observe the posted speed limits**, which can be as low as 20 kph (12 mph).

SAFETY ON THE ROAD

The mythical *banditos* are not a big concern in Baja. Still, **never drive at night**, especially in rural areas. Cows and burros grazing alongside the road can pose a real danger—you never know when they'll decide to wander into traffic. Other good reasons for not driving at night include potholes, cars with no working lights, road-hogging trucks, and difficulty with getting assistance. Plan driving times, and if night is falling, find a nearby hotel.

Though it isn't common in Los Cabos, police may pull you over for supposedly breaking the law, or for being a good prospect for a scam. If it happens to you, remember to **be polite**—displays of anger will only make matters worse—and be aware that a police officer might be pulling you over for something you didn't do. Corruption is a fact of life in Mexico, and the $5 it costs to get your license back is definitely supplementary income for the officer who pulled you over with no intention of taking you to police headquarters.

If you are stopped for speeding, the officer is supposed to hold your license until you pay the fine at the local police station. But he will always prefer taking a *mordida* (small bribe) to wasting his time at the police station. If you decide to dispute a preposterous charge, do so with a smile, and tell the officer that you would like to talk to the police captain when you get to the station. The officer usually will let you go.

Children in Los Cabos

Most people are happy to see kids and will do all they can to be of assistance. If you are renting a car, don't forget to **arrange for a car seat** when you reserve. For general advice about traveling with children, consult *Fodor's FYI: Travel with Your Baby* (available in bookstores everywhere).

FOOD
Grocery stores in Los Cabos carry a limited supply of U.S. brands familiar to children. Several franchise restaurants, including McDonald's, Domino's Pizza, Dairy Queen, Hard Rock Cafe, and Johnny Rockets, have locations in Cabo San Lucas.

LODGING
Most hotels in Los Cabos allow children under a certain age to stay in their parents' room at no extra charge, but others charge for them as extra adults; be sure to **find out the cutoff age for children's discounts.** The hotels on Playa Médano have plenty of family-oriented activities on the beach. The Pueblo Bonito Rosé is especially family friendly. Other good choices are the Hotel Hacienda in San Lucas and the Westin Regina Resort in the Corridor. The Presidente Inter-Continental in San José del Cabo may be one of the best places for families: the all-inclusive policies include a children's program, baby-sitting services, and unlimited kids' food.

PRECAUTIONS
Los Cabos is generally as safe as the U.S. for children, but Mexico has extremely strict policies about children entering the country. All children under the age of 18, including infants, are considered minors and must have proof of citizenship. A birth certificate is sufficient. Minors traveling with a single parent

must have a notarized letter from the other parent stating that the child is allowed to enter Mexico. If a child is traveling alone or with someone other than his/her parents, he or she must have a notarized consent form signed by both parents. Airlines also require the name, address, and telephone number of the person meeting an unaccompanied minor upon arrival in Mexico. If one parent is deceased or the child has only one legal parent, a notarized statement to this effect must be presented. Parents must fill out a tourist card for each child over the age of 10.

SUPPLIES & EQUIPMENT

Basic supplies are readily available, though you might not find the brands you prefer. Imported diapers and a few brands of baby food are available in grocery stores. Prices are higher than in the United States.

Customs & Duties

When shopping abroad, keep receipts for all purchases. Upon reentering the country, **be ready to show customs officials what you've bought.** Pack purchases together in an easily accessible place. If you think a duty is incorrect, appeal the assessment. If you object to the way your clearance was handled, note the inspector's badge number. In either case, first ask to see a supervisor. If the problem isn't resolved, write to the appropriate authorities, beginning with the port director at your point of entry.

IN AUSTRALIA

Australian residents who are 18 or older may bring home A$400 worth of souvenirs and gifts (including jewelry), 250 cigarettes or 250 grams of cigars or other tobacco products, and 1,125 ml of alcohol (including wine, beer, and spirits). Residents under 18 may bring back A$200 worth of goods. Members of the same family traveling together may pool their allowances. Prohibited items include meat products. Seeds, plants, and fruits need to be declared upon arrival.

➤INFORMATION: **Australian Customs Service** (Regional Director, Box 8, Sydney, NSW 2001, tel. 02/9213–2000 or 1300/363263, 02/9364–7222 or 1800/020–504 quarantine-inquiry line, fax 02/9213–4043, www.customs.gov.au).

IN CANADA

Canadian residents who have been out of Canada for at least seven days may bring in C$750 worth of goods duty-free. If you've been away fewer than seven days but more than 48 hours, the duty-free allowance drops to C$200. If your trip lasts 24 to 48 hours, the allowance is C$50. You may not pool allowances with family members. Goods claimed under the C$750 exemption may follow you by mail; those claimed under the lesser exemptions must accompany you. Alcohol and tobacco products may be included in the seven-day and 48-hour exemptions but not in the 24-hour exemption. If you meet the age requirements of the province or territory through which you reenter Canada, you may bring in, duty-free, 1.5 liters of wine or 1.14 liters (40 imperial ounces) of liquor or 24 12-ounce cans or bottles of beer or ale. Also, if you meet the local age requirement for tobacco products, you may bring in, duty-free, 200 cigarettes and 50 cigars. Check ahead of time with the Canada Customs and Revenue Agency or the Department of Agriculture for policies regarding meat products, seeds, plants, and fruits.

You may send an unlimited number of gifts (only one gift per recipient, however) worth up to C$60 each duty-free to Canada. Label the package UNSOLICITED GIFT—VALUE UNDER $60. Alcohol and tobacco are excluded.

➤INFORMATION: **Canada Customs and Revenue Agency** (2265 St. Laurent Blvd., Ottawa, Ontario K1G 4K3, tel. 800/461–9999 in Canada, 204/983–3500, 506/636–5064, www.ccra.gc.ca).

IN NEW ZEALAND

All homeward-bound residents may bring back NZ$700 worth of souvenirs and gifts; passengers may not pool their allowances, and children can claim only the concession on goods intended for their own use. For those 17 or older, the duty-free allowance also includes 4.5 liters of wine or beer; one 1,125-ml bottle of spirits; and either 200 cigarettes, 250 grams of tobacco, 50 cigars, or a combination of the three up to 250 grams. Meat products, seeds, plants, and fruits must be declared upon arrival to the Agricultural Services Department.

➤INFORMATION: **New Zealand Customs** (Head office: The Customhouse, 17–21 Whitmore St., Box 2218, Wellington, tel. 09/300–5399 or 0800/428–786, www.customs.govt.nz).

IN THE U.K.

From countries outside the European Union, including Mexico, you may bring home, duty-free, 200 cigarettes, 50 cigars, 100 cigarillos, or 250 grams of tobacco; 1 liter of spirits or 2 liters of fortified or sparkling wine or liqueurs; 2 liters of still table wine; 60 ml of perfume; 250 ml of toilet water; plus £145 worth of other goods, including gifts and souvenirs. Prohibited items include meat and dairy products, seeds, plants, and fruits.

➤INFORMATION: **HM Customs and Excise** (Portcullis House, 21 Cowbridge Rd. E, Cardiff CF11 9SS, tel. 0845/010–9000 or 0208/929–0152 advice service, 0208/929–6731 or 0208/910–3602 complaints, www.hmce.gov.uk).

IN THE U.S.

U.S. residents who have been out of the country for at least 48 hours may bring home, for personal use, $800 worth of foreign goods duty-free, as long as they haven't used the $800 allowance or any part of it in the past 30 days. This exemption may include 1 liter of alcohol (for travelers 21 and older), 200 cigarettes, and 100 non-Cuban cigars. Family members from the same household who are traveling together may pool their $800 personal exemptions. For fewer than 48 hours, the duty-free allowance drops to $200, which may include 50 cigarettes, 10 non-Cuban cigars, and 150 ml of alcohol (or 150 ml of perfume containing alcohol). The $200 allowance cannot be combined with other individuals' exemptions, and if you exceed it, the full value of all the goods will be taxed. Antiques, which U.S. Customs and Border Protection defines as objects more than 100 years old, enter duty-free, as do original works of art done entirely by hand, including paintings, drawings, and sculptures. This doesn't apply to folk art or handicrafts, which are in general dutiable.

You may also send packages home duty-free, with a limit of one parcel per addressee per day (except alcohol or tobacco products or perfume worth more than $5). You can mail up to $200 worth of goods for personal use; label the package PERSONAL USE and attach a list of its contents and their retail value. If the package contains your used personal belongings, mark it AMERICAN GOODS RETURNED to avoid paying duties. You may send up to $100 worth of goods as a gift; mark the package UNSOLICITED GIFT. Mailed items do not affect your duty-free allowance on your return.

To avoid paying duty on foreign-made high-ticket items you already own and will take on your trip, register them with Customs before you leave the country. Consider filing a Certificate of Registration for laptops, cameras, watches, and other digital devices identified with serial numbers or other permanent markings; you can keep the certificate for other trips. Otherwise, bring a sales receipt or insurance form to show that you owned the item before you left the United States.

For more about duties, restricted items, and other information about international travel, check out U.S. Customs and Border Protection's online brochure, *Know Before You Go*.

➤INFORMATION: U.S. Bureau of Customs and Border Protection (for inquiries and equipment registration, 1300 Pennsylvania Ave. NW, Washington, DC 20229, www.cbp.gov, tel. 877/287–8667, 202/354–1000; for complaints, Customer Satisfaction Unit, 1300 Pennsylvania Ave. NW, Room 5.2C, Washington, DC 20229).

Disabilities & Accessibility

Los Cabos is poorly equipped for travelers with disabilities. Public transportation is not wheelchair accessible, and roads and sidewalks are often crowded. People on the street will usually assist you if you ask. You cannot rent vehicles outfitted for travelers with disabilities in Los Cabos, so **bring a specially equipped car or van.**

Most hotels and restaurants have at least a few steps, and although rooms considered "wheelchair accessible" by hotel owners are usually on the ground floor, the doorways and bathroom may not be maneuverable. Call ahead to find out what a hotel or restaurant can offer.

RESERVATIONS

When discussing accessibility with an operator or reservations agent, ask hard questions. Are there any stairs, inside or out? Are there grab bars next to the toilet *and* in the shower/tub? How wide is the doorway to the room? To the bathroom? For the most extensive facilities meeting the latest legal specifications, opt for newer accommodations. If you reserve through a toll-free number, consider also calling the hotel's local number to confirm the information from the central reservations office. Get confirmation in writing when you can.

Electricity

For U.S. and Canadian travelers, electrical converters are not necessary because Mexico operates on the 60-cycle, 120-volt system; however, many Mexican outlets have not been updated to accommodate three-prong and polarized plugs (those with one larger prong), so to be safe **bring an adapter.** If your appliances are dual-voltage you'll need only an adapter. Don't use 110-volt outlets, marked FOR SHAVERS ONLY, for high-wattage appliances such as blow dryers. Most laptops operate equally well on 110 and 220 volts and so require only an adapter.

Embassies & Consulates

➤**AUSTRALIA: Australian Embassy** (Rubén Darío 55, Col. Polanco, Mexico City, tel. 5531–5225).

➤**CANADA: Canadian Consulate** (Plaza José Green, Blvd. Mijares, San José del Cabo, tel. 624/142–4333). **Canadian Embassy** (Schiller 529, Colonia Rincon del Bosque, Mexico City, tel. 5724–7900).

➤**NEW ZEALAND: New Zealand Embassy** (José Luis LaGrange 103, 10th fl., Col. Polanco, Mexico City, tel. 5281–5486).

➤**UNITED KINGDOM: British Embassy** (Río Lerma 71, Col. Cuauhtémoc, Mexico City, tel. 5207–2089).

➤**UNITED STATES: U.S. Embassy** (Paseo de la Reforma 305, Col. Cuauhtémoc, Mexico City, tel. 5209–9100).

Emergencies

You're not protected by the laws of your native land once you're on Mexican soil. If you get into a scrape with the law, you can call the Citizens' Emergency Center in Washington, D.C., open weekdays 8:15 AM–10 PM EST, Saturday 9–3. You can also call the 24-hour English-language hotline of the Procuraduría de Protecciónal Turista (Attorney General for the Protection of Tourists) in Mexico City; it can provide immediate assistance as well as general, nonemergency guidance. **In an emergency, dial 060 from any phone.**

For medical emergencies, Tourist Medical Assist has English-speaking physicians who make emergency calls around the clock.

►**DOCTORS & DENTISTS: Tourist Medical Assist** (Morelos, between Niños Héroes and 16 de Septiembre, Cabo San Lucas, tel. 624/143–5404; Paseo Finisterra s/n, San José del Cabo, tel. 624/142–0999). **Dental office** (Av. Cárdenas, across from the Hotel Mar de Cortés, Cabo San Lucas, tel. 624/143–0579).

►**EMERGENCY SERVICES: Highway Patrol** (San José del Cabo, tel. 624/146–0573). **Police** (tel. 624/142–2835 in San José del Cabo, 624/143–3977 in Cabo San Lucas). **Procuraduría de Protección al Turista** (Attorney General for the Protection of the Tourist, tel. 01–800/903–9200, 800/482–9832 from the U.S.).

►**HOSPITALS: I.M.S.S. Hospital** (Doblado, between Márques de León and Carretera Transpeninsular, San José del Cabo, tel. 624/142–0180). **I.M.S.S. Hospital** (Hwy. 19, Cabo San Lucas, tel. 624/143–1444).

Gay & Lesbian Travel

Though overt harassment is uncommon in Los Cabos, Mexican same-sex couples keep a low profile, and it's a good idea for foreign same-sex couples to do the same. Two people of the same gender can often have a hard time getting a *cama matrimonial* (double bed) in smaller hotels. Larger resorts or chain hotels are usually more receptive.

►**Gay- & Lesbian-Friendly Travel Agencies: Different Roads Travel** (8383 Wilshire Blvd., Suite 520, Beverly Hills, CA 90211, tel. 323/651–5557 or 800/429–8747 [Ext. 14 for both], fax 323/651–5454). **Kennedy Travel** (130 W. 42nd St., Suite 401, New York, NY 10036, tel. 212/840–8659, 800/237–7433, fax 212/730–2269, www.kennedytravel.com). **Now, Voyager** (4406 18th St.,

San Francisco, CA 94114, tel. 415/626–1169 or 800/255–6951, fax 415/626–8626, www.nowvoyager.com). **Skylink Travel and Tour/Flying Dutchmen Travel** (1455 N. Dutton Ave., Suite A, Santa Rosa, CA 95401, tel. 707/546–9888 or 800/225–5759, fax 707/636–0951), serving lesbian travelers.

Health

DIVERS' ALERT
Do not fly within 24 hours of scuba diving.

FOOD & DRINK
In general, Los Cabos does not impose as great a health risk as other parts of Mexico may. Nevertheless, **watch what you eat** and **drink only bottled water** or water that has been boiled for a few minutes. Water in most major hotels is safe for brushing your teeth, but to avoid any risk, use bottled water. Hotels with water-purification systems will post signs to that effect in the rooms.

When ordering cold drinks at establishments that don't seem to get many tourists, **skip the ice:** *sin hielo.* (You can usually identify ice made commercially from purified water by its uniform shape.)

Stay away from uncooked food and unpasteurized milk and milk products. *Tacos al pastor*—thin pork slices grilled on a spit and garnished with the usual cilantro, onions, and chili peppers—are delicious but dangerous. It's also a good idea to pass up *ceviche*, raw fish cured in lemon juice—a favorite appetizer, especially at seaside resorts. The Mexican Department of Health warns that marinating in lemon juice does not constitute the "cooking" that would make the shellfish safe to eat. Be wary of hamburgers sold from street stands, because you can never be certain what meat they are made with. That said, many travelers eat ceviche, street-stand tacos, and all the other wonderful foods that make dining in Mexico fun. If you're dining in a clean hotel or tourist-oriented restaurant, be a bit more adventuresome. Some travelers take a spoonful of Pepto-Bismol before eating as a precaution.

The major health risk, known as *turista*, or traveler's diarrhea, is caused by eating contaminated fruit or vegetables or drinking contaminated water. Mild cases may respond to Imodium (known generically as loperamide or Lomotil) or Pepto-Bismol, both of which can be purchased over the counter. Do not take Imodium or other anti-diarrheal drugs for more than a day or two. If they don't cure the problem by then, you should definitely see a doctor. Drink plenty of purified water or tea; chamomile tea (*te de manzanilla*) is a good folk remedy and it's readily available in restaurants throughout Mexico. In severe cases, rehydrate yourself with Gatorade or a salt-sugar solution (¼ teaspoon salt and 4 tablespoons sugar per quart of water).

PESTS & OTHER HAZARDS

Caution is advised when venturing out in the Mexican sun. Sunbathers lulled by a slightly overcast sky or the sea breezes can be burned badly in just 20 minutes. To avoid overexposure, **use strong sunscreens and avoid the peak sun hours** of noon–2 PM. Sunscreen, including many U.S. brands, can be found in pharmacies, supermarkets, and resort gift shops in Los Cabos.

SHOTS & MEDICATIONS

No special shots or vaccinations are required for Los Cabos. No cases of malaria have been reported in Los Cabos.

Holidays & Festivals

Mexico is the land of festivals; if you reserve lodging well in advance, they present a golden opportunity to have a thoroughly Mexican experience. Banks and government offices close during Holy Week (the week leading to Easter Sunday) and on Cinco de Mayo, Día de la Raza, and Independence Day. Government offices usually have reduced hours and staff from

Christmas through New Year's Day. Some banks and offices close for religious holidays.

Official holidays include New Year's Day (Jan. 1); Constitution Day (Feb. 5); Benito Juárez's Birthday (Mar. 21); Good Friday (Friday before Easter Sunday); Easter Sunday (Mar. 27, 2005; Apr. 16, 2006); Labor Day (May 1); Cinco de Mayo (May 5); St. John the Baptist Day (June 24); Independence Day (Sept. 16); Día de la Raza (Day of the Race; Oct. 12); Dia de los Muertos (Day of the Dead; Nov. 2); Anniversary of the Mexican Revolution (Nov. 20); Christmas (Dec. 25).

Festivals include Carnaval (Feb.–Mar., before Lent); Semana Santa (Holy Week; week before Easter Sunday); Día de Nuestra Señora de Guadalupe (Day of Our Lady of Guadalupe; Dec. 12); and Las Posadas (pre-Christmas religious celebrations; Dec. 16–25).

Language

Although Spanish is the official language of Mexico, you may hear more English on the streets of Los Cabos. Indian languages are spoken by approximately 20% of the population, principally on the mainland. Basic English is widely understood by most people employed in tourism, less so in the less developed areas. At the very least, shopkeepers will know the numbers for bargaining purposes.

As in most other foreign countries, knowing the mother tongue has a way of opening doors, so **learn some Spanish words and phrases.** Mexicans welcome even the most halting attempts to use the language.

Castilian Spanish—which is different from Latin American Spanish not only in pronunciation and grammar but also in vocabulary—is most widely taught outside Mexico. Words or phrases that are harmless or everyday in one country can offend in another. Unless you are lucky enough to be briefed on these nuances by a native coach, the only way to learn is by trial and error.

LANGUAGES FOR TRAVELERS
A phrase book and language-tape set can help get you started. *Fodor's Spanish for Travelers* (available at bookstores everywhere) is excellent.

Mail & Shipping

The Mexican postal system is slow and unreliable, but it is improving. Still, **never send valuable packages through the mail** or expect to receive them, as they may be lost. (For emergencies, use a courier service or the express-mail service, with insurance). If you are an American Express cardholder, your best bet is to send a package to the AmEx office nearest the recipient.

Letters mailed from Los Cabos travel by airmail but may take up to two weeks to reach their destination. The *oficina de correo* (post office) in San José del Cabo is open 8–7 weekdays (with a possible closure for lunch) and 9–1 Saturday. The Cabo San Lucas post office is open 9–1 and 3–6 weekdays, 9–noon Saturday.

EXPRESS SERVICES
Federal Express doesn't serve Baja California Sur (the FedEx office closest to Los Cabos is in Tijuana). DHL has express service (overnight service isn't available) for letters and packages from Los Cabos to the United States, Australia, Canada, New Zealand, and the United Kingdom; most deliveries take three to four days. To the United States, letters take three days and boxes and packages take four days. Cabo San Lucas and San José del Cabo each have a DHL drop-off location. Mail Boxes Etc. can help with DHL, UPS and postal services.

►**MAJOR SERVICES: American Express** (Tourcabos, Plaza Los Cabos, Zona Turística, San José del Cabo, tel. 624/142–1306; Tourcabos, Hotel Pueblo Bonito, Av. Playa del Médano, Cabo San Lucas, tel. 624/143–2787). **DHL Worldwide Express** (Plaza los Portales, Hwy. 1, Km 31.5, Local 2, San José del Cabo, tel. 624/142–2148; Hwy. 1, Km 1, Centro Comercial Plaza Copan, Local 18 & 21, Cabo San Lucas, tel. 624/143–5202, 624/143–1430). **Mail Boxes Etc.** (Plaza las Palmas, San José del Cabo, tel. 624/142–3032; Blvd. Marina, Plaza Bonita Local 44-E, Cabo San Lucas, tel. 624/143–3032).

►**POST OFFICES: Cabo San Lucas Oficina de Correo** (Av. Lázaro Cárdenas s/n, no phone). **San José del Cabo Oficina de Correo** (Mijares and Margarita Maya de Juárez, no phone).

POSTAL RATES
It costs 6 pesos (about 60¢) to send a postcard or letter weighing under 20 grams to the United States, 8 pesos (about 80¢) to Canada or Great Britain.

RECEIVING MAIL
To receive mail in Mexico, you can have it sent to your hotel or use *poste restante* at the post office. In the latter case, the address must include the words "a/c Lista de Correos" (general delivery), followed by the city, state, postal code, and country. To use this service, you must first register with the post office at which you wish to receive your mail. The post office posts and updates daily a list of names for whom mail has been received.

Holders of American Express cards can have mail (letters only) sent to them in care of the local American Express office. For a list of offices worldwide, write for the *Traveler's Companion* from **American Express** (Box 678, Canal Street Station, New York, NY 10013).

INTERNET SERVICES

Cabo Mail Internet in Cabo San Lucas has several computers and charges $10 an hour. Cabocafe in San José del Cabo offers access for $9 an hour.

➤INTERNET CAFÉS: **Cabocafe** (Plaza José Green, Suite 3, Blvd. Mijares, San José del Cabo, tel. 624/142–5250). **Cabo Mail Internet** (Blvd. Cárdenas, Cabo San Lucas, tel. 624/143–3797).

Money Matters

Mexico has a reputation for being inexpensive, but Los Cabos is one of the most expensive places to visit. Prices rise from 10% to 18% annually and are comparable to those in southern California.

Prices in this book are quoted most often in U.S. dollars because the value of the currency fluctuates considerably; what costs 90 pesos today might cost 120 pesos in six months. U.S. dollars are readily accepted in Los Cabos. Prices throughout this guide are given for adults. Substantially reduced fees are almost always available for children, students, and senior citizens. For information on taxes, *see* Taxes.

ATMS

ATMs (*cajas automáticas*) are commonplace in Los Cabos, and some dispense dollars and pesos. Cirrus and Plus cards are the most commonly accepted. Before you leave home, **ask what the transaction fee will be** for withdrawing money in Mexico. (It's usually $3 a pop.) Many Mexican ATMs cannot accept PINs (personal identification numbers; *números de clave*) that have more than four digits; if yours is longer, **ask your bank about changing your PIN before you leave home,** and keep in mind that processing such a change often takes a few weeks.

For cash advances, plan to use Visa or MasterCard, as many Mexican ATMs don't accept American Express. The ATMs at Banamex, one of the oldest nationwide banks, tend to be the most reliable. Bancomer is another bank with many ATM locations, but they usually provide only cash advances. Serfín banks have reliable ATMs that accept credit cards as well as Plus and Cirrus cards.

CREDIT CARDS

Traveler's checks and all major U.S. credit cards are accepted in much of Los Cabos. Smaller, less expensive restaurants and shops, however, tend to take only cash. In general, credit cards aren't accepted in small towns and villages, except for tourist-oriented hotels. Diners Club is usually accepted only in major hotel chains; the most widely accepted cards are MasterCard and Visa. When shopping, you can usually get better prices if you pay with cash.

At the same time, when traveling internationally you will receive wholesale exchange rates when you make purchases with credit cards. These exchange rates are usually better than rates that banks give you for changing money. In Los Cabos the decision to pay cash or to use a credit card might depend on whether the establishment in which you are making a purchase finds bargaining for prices acceptable. To avoid fraud, it's wise to make sure that "pesos" is clearly marked on all credit-card receipts.

Throughout this guide, the following abbreviations are used: **AE**, American Express; **DC**, Diners Club; **MC**, MasterCard; and **V**, Visa.

CURRENCY

At this writing, exchange rates are 11 pesos to US$1; 8.30 pesos to C$1; 20.75 pesos to £1; 8.66 pesos to A$1; and 7.65 pesos to NZ$1. Check with your bank or the financial pages of your local newspaper for current exchange rates. For quick estimates of how much something costs in U.S. dollars, divide prices given in pesos by 10. For example, 50 pesos would be about $5.

Mexican currency comes in denominations of 20-, 50-, 100-, 200-, 500-, and 1,000-peso bills. Coins come in denominations of 1, 2, 5, 10, and 20 pesos and 5, 10, 20, and 50 centavos. Centavo coins are still in circulation but are virtually worthless. Many of the coins and bills are very similar in appearance, so check carefully.

CURRENCY EXCHANGE

ATM currency-exchange rates are the best of all because they are based on wholesale rates offered only by major banks. And if you take out a fair amount of cash per withdrawal, the transaction fee becomes less of a strike against the exchange rate (in percentage terms). However, most ATMs allow only up to $150 a transaction. Banks and *casas de cambio* (money-exchange houses) have the second-best exchange rates. The difference from one place to another is usually only a few centavos. Bank rates are regulated by the federal government and are therefore invariable, although casas de cambio have slightly more-variable rates. Some hotels also exchange money, but for providing you with this convenience they help themselves to a bigger commission than banks. You can do well at most airport exchange booths, but not necessarily at bus stations or in hotels, restaurants, or stores.

When changing money, count your bills before leaving the bank or casa de cambio, and don't take any partially torn or taped-together notes; they won't be accepted anywhere. Also, be careful to bring unmarked bills with you. Any torn, marked, or otherwise worn bills might not be accepted. Many shop and restaurant owners are unable to make change for large bills. Enough of these encounters may compel you to request *billetes chicos* (small bills) when you exchange money.

►**EXCHANGE SERVICES: International Currency Express** (tel. 888/278–6628, www.foreignmoney.com). **Thomas Cook Currency Services** (tel. 800/287–7362, www.us.thomascook. com).

Packing

In your carry-on luggage, pack an extra pair of eyeglasses or contact lenses and enough of any medication you take to last a few days longer than the entire trip. You may also ask your doctor to write a spare prescription using the drug's generic name, as brand names may vary from country to country. In luggage to be checked, **never pack prescription drugs, valuables, or undeveloped film.** And don't forget to carry with you the addresses of offices that handle refunds of lost traveler's checks. Check *Fodor's How to Pack* (available at online retailers and bookstores everywhere) for more tips.

To avoid customs and security delays, carry medications in their original packaging. Don't pack any sharp objects in your carry-on luggage, including knives of any size or material, scissors, nail clippers, and corkscrews, or anything else that might arouse suspicion.

To avoid having your checked luggage chosen for hand inspection, don't cram bags full. The U.S. Transportation Security Administration suggests packing shoes on top and placing personal items you don't want touched in clear plastic bags.

Passports & Visas

When traveling internationally, carry your passport even if you don't need one (it's always the best form of I.D.) and **make two photocopies of the data page** (one for someone at home and another for you, carried separately from your passport). If you lose your passport, promptly call the nearest embassy or consulate and the local police.

U.S. passport applications for children under age 14 require consent from both parents or legal guardians; both parents must appear together to sign the application. If only one parent appears, he or she must submit a written statement from the other parent authorizing passport issuance for the child. A parent with sole authority must present evidence of it when applying; acceptable documentation includes the child's certified birth certificate listing only the applying parent, a court order specifically permitting this parent's travel with the child, or a death certificate for the nonapplying parent. Application forms and instructions are available on the Web site of the U.S. State Department's Bureau of Consular Affairs (travel.state.gov.).

ENTERING MEXICO

For stays of up to 180 days, Americans must **prove citizenship through either a valid passport, certified copy of a birth certificate, or voter-registration card** (the last two must be accompanied by a government-issue photo ID). Minors traveling with one parent need notarized permission from the absent parent. For stays of more than 180 days, all U.S. citizens, even infants, need a valid passport to enter Mexico. Minors also need parental permission.

Canadians need only proof of citizenship to enter Mexico for stays of up to six months. U.K. citizens need only a valid passport to enter Mexico for stays of up to three months.

At this writing, Mexico has instituted a fee of about US$22 that applies to all visitors except those who stay less than 72 hours and those who do not stray past the 26- to 30-km (16- to 18-mi) checkpoint south of the U.S.–Mexico border. If you're entering Mexico by car, pick up a form at the border and turn it in with the fee at a Mexican bank. If you're arriving by air, the fee is usually tacked on to the airline-ticket price. You must pay the fee each time you extend your 30-day tourist visa.

Restrooms

Expect to find clean flushing toilets, toilet tissue, soap, and running water in Los Cabos. Other places should have simple but clean toilets. An exception may be small roadside stands or restaurants in rural areas. If there is a bucket and a large container of water sitting outside the facilities, fill the bucket and use it for the flush. Some public places, such as bus stations, charge one or two pesos for use of the facility, but toilet paper is included in the fee. Still, it's always a good idea to carry some tissue. Throw your toilet paper and any other materials into trash cans rather than the toilet in small businesses and remote areas that may have poor plumbing.

Safety

Although the Los Cabos area is one of the safest in Mexico, it is still important to be aware of your surroundings and to follow normal safety precautions. Everyone has heard some horror story about highway assaults, pickpocketing, bribes, or foreigners languishing in Mexican jails. Reports of these crimes apply in large part to Mexico City and other large cities; in Los Cabos, pickpocketing is usually the biggest concern.

Don't wear a money belt or a waist pack, both of which peg you as a tourist. Distribute your cash and any valuables (including your credit cards and passport) between a deep front pocket, an inside jacket or vest pocket, and a hidden money pouch. Do not reach for the money pouch once you're in public.

Women traveling alone in the beach and resort areas of Los Cabos usually do not have any problems. If you are on the streets or in bars at night, you might encounter more trouble from male tourists than from locals. However, women are sometimes subjected to *piropos* (catcalls). To avoid this, try not to wear tight or provocative clothing or enter street bars or cantinas alone; in some very conservative rural areas, even sleeveless shirts or

Bermuda shorts may seem inappropriate to the locals. Your best strategy is always to try to ignore the offender, do not speak to him, and go on about your business. If the situation seems to be getting out of hand, do not hesitate to ask someone for help. Piropos are one thing, but outright harassment of women is not considered acceptable behavior. If you express outrage, you should find no shortage of willing defenders.

Taxes

Mexico charges an airport departure tax of about US$12 or the peso equivalent for international and domestic flights. This tax is usually included in the price of your ticket, but check to be certain. Traveler's checks and credit cards are not accepted at the airport as payment for this fee.

A 2% tax on accommodations is charged in Los Cabos, with proceeds used for tourism promotion.

VALUE-ADDED TAX

Baja California Sur has a value-added tax of 10%, called I.V.A. (*impuesto de valor agregado*), which is occasionally (and illegally) waived for cash purchases. Other taxes and charges apply for phone calls made from your hotel room.

Taxis

Government-certified taxis have a license with a photo of the driver and a taxi number prominently displayed. In Los Cabos, two unions control all taxis: red or yellow cabs are from San José and blue-and-black or green-and-gray cabs are from Cabo San Lucas. Most taxis are large American sedans or vans. Taxis charge according to the distance; be sure to agree on a fare before getting in. Taxis are readily available at hotels, tourist attractions, and on the street. Tipping is not necessary unless the driver helps you with your bags, in which case a few pesos are appropriate.

Taxis are plentiful but expensive in Los Cabos. (If you are not renting a car, you will find that public bus transportation is a reliable alternative when traveling between San José del Cabo and Cabo San Lucas. If you're considering a day trip by bus to Todos Santos or La Paz, though, note that the cost of a cab from Corridor hotels to the bus station may be nearly as much as a car rental!) In most cases you will be staying within walking distance of a beach.

From the airport, book your taxi at the taxi booth, which ensures that your fare is established beforehand. As in any airport, don't leave your luggage unattended while making transportation arrangements.

Telephones

Los Cabos has good telephone service, with pay phone booths along the streets and the Corridor. Most phones have Touch-Tone (digital) circuitry. Phone numbers in Mexico change frequently; a recording may offer the new number, so it's useful to learn the Spanish words for numbers 1 through 9. Beware of pay phones and hotel-room phones with signs saying "Call Home" and other enticements. Some of these phone companies charge astronomical rates.

AREA & COUNTRY CODES

The country code for Mexico is 52. When calling a Mexico number from abroad, dial the country code and then the area code and local number. Area codes in Mexico changed twice in 2001, creating massive confusion. At this writing, the area code for all of Los Cabos is 624. All local numbers now have seven digits. Many published materials have the old area codes (either 114 or simply 1) followed by a five-digit local number. When calling from outside Los Cabos, you can usually get the right number by dialing the new area code (624) plus the old area code minus the first 1, then dial the old local number. One benefit to the change is that all calls within Los Cabos are now toll-free.

DIRECTORY & OPERATOR ASSISTANCE

Directory assistance in Mexico is 040 nationwide. For international assistance, dial 020 first for an international operator and most likely you'll get one who speaks English; indicate in which city, state, and country you require directory assistance and you will be connected with directory assistance there.

INTERNATIONAL CALLS

To make a call to the United States or Canada, dial 001 before the area code and number; to call Europe, South Africa, Australia, or New Zealand, dial 00 before the country and city codes. The country code for the U.K. is 44, Australia is 61, New Zealand is 64, and South Africa is 27. For operator assistance in making an international call dial 090.

LOCAL & LONG-DISTANCE CALLS

For local or long-distance calls, one option is to find a *caseta de larga distancia,* a telephone service usually operated out of a small business; look for the phone symbol on the door. Casetas have become less common as pay phones have begun to appear even in the smallest towns. Rates at casetas seem to vary widely, so shop around. Sometimes you can make collect calls from casetas, and sometimes you cannot, depending on the operator and possibly your degree of visible desperation. Casetas generally charge 50¢–$1.50 to place a collect call (some charge by the minute); it's usually better to call *por cobrar* (collect) from a pay phone.

LONG-DISTANCE SERVICES

AT&T, MCI, and Sprint access codes make calling long-distance relatively convenient, but you may find the local access number blocked in many hotel rooms. First ask the hotel operator to connect you. If the hotel operator balks, ask for an international operator, or dial the international operator yourself. One way to improve your odds of getting connected to your long-distance carrier is to travel with more than one company's calling card (a hotel may block Sprint, for example, but not MCI). If all else fails, call from a pay phone.

➤**ACCESS CODES: AT&T Direct** (tel. 01–800/462–4240). **MCI WorldPhone** (tel. 01–800/674–7000). **Sprint International Access** (tel. 01–800/877–8000).

PUBLIC PHONES

Occasionally you'll see traditional black, square pay phones with push buttons or dials; although they have a coin slot on top, local calls are free. However, these coin-only pay phones are usually broken. Newer pay phones have an unmarked slot for prepaid phone cards called Telmex cards. The cards are sold in 30-, 50-, or 100-peso denominations at newsstands or pharmacies. Credit is deleted from the Telmex card as you use it, and your balance is displayed on a small screen on the phone. Some phones have two unmarked slots, one for a Telmex card and the other for a credit card. These are primarily for Mexican bank cards, but some accept Visa or MasterCard.

TOLL-FREE NUMBERS

Toll-free numbers in Mexico start with an 800 prefix. To reach them, you need to dial 01 before the number. In this guide, Mexico-only toll-free numbers appear as follows: 01–800/123–4567 (numbers have seven digits). Most of the 800 numbers in this book work in the U.S. only and are listed simply: 800/123–4567; you cannot access a U.S. 800 number from Mexico. Some U.S. toll-free numbers ring directly at Mexican properties. Don't be deterred if someone answers the phone in Spanish. Simply ask for someone who speaks English. Toll-free numbers that work in other countries are labeled accordingly.

Time

Baja California Sur is on Mountain Standard Time.

Tipping

When tipping in Los Cabos, remember that the minimum wage is the equivalent of $3 a day and that the vast majority of workers in the tourist industry live barely above the poverty line. However, there are Mexicans who think in dollars and know, for example, that in the United States porters are tipped about $2 a bag; many of them expect the peso equivalent from foreigners but are sometimes happy to accept 5 pesos (about 5¢) a bag from Mexicans. They will complain either verbally or with a facial expression if they feel they deserve more—you and your conscience must decide. Following are some guidelines. Naturally, larger tips are always welcome.

For porters and bellboys at airports and at moderate and inexpensive hotels, $1 per bag should be sufficient. At expensive hotels, porters expect at least $2 per bag. Leave $1 per night for maids at all hotels. The norm for waiters is 10% to 15% of the bill, depending on service (make sure a 10%–15% service charge hasn't already been added to the bill, although this practice is more common in resorts). Tipping taxi drivers is necessary only if the driver helps with your bags; 50¢ to $1 should be enough, depending on the extent of the help. Tip tour guides and drivers at least $1 per half day or 10% of the tour fee, minimum. Gas-station attendants receive 30¢ to 50¢, more if they check the oil, tires, etc. Parking attendants—including those at restaurants with valet parking—should be tipped 50¢ to $1.

Travel Agencies

A good travel agent puts your needs first. Look for an agency that has been in business at least five years, emphasizes customer service, and has someone on staff who specializes in your destination. In addition, **make sure the agency belongs to a professional trade organization.** The American Society of Travel Agents (ASTA)—the largest and most influential in the field with more than 20,000 members in some 140 countries—maintains and enforces a strict code of ethics and will step in to help mediate any agent-client disputes involving ASTA members if necessary. ASTA (whose motto is "Without a travel agent, you're on your own") also maintains a Web site that includes a directory of agents.

➤**LOCAL AGENT REFERRALS: American Society of Travel Agents** (ASTA) 1101 King St., Suite 200, Alexandria, VA 22314, tel. 703/739–2782 or 800/965–2782 24-hr hotline, fax 703/684–8319, www.astanet.com). **Association of British Travel Agents** (68–71 Newman St., London W1T 3AH, tel. 020/7637–2444, fax 020/7637–0713, www.abta.com). **Association of Canadian Travel Agencies** (130 Albert St., Suite 1705, Ottawa, Ontario K1P 5G4, tel. 613/237–3657, fax 613/237–7052, www.acta.ca). **Australian Federation of Travel Agents** (Level 3, 309 Pitt St., Sydney, NSW 2000, tel. 02/9264–3299 or 1300/363–416, fax 02/9264–1085, www.afta.com.au). **Travel Agents' Association of New Zealand** (Level 5, Tourism and Travel House, 79 Boulcott St., Box 1888, Wellington 6001, tel. 04/499–0104, fax 04/499–0786, www.taanz.org.nz).

Visitor Information

The Mexican-government tourist office and the private travel sector have joined together to form a national tourist and promotion board, so the best way to get information is via the toll-free number that connects you to the promotion office in Mexico City (operators speak English). The Los Cabos municipal government created a tourism office in 2003; at this writing, their offices had not yet opened to the public, but you can reach staff by phone or get information online. Otherwise, your hotel tour desk is always a good source. Avoid tour stands on the streets; they are usually associated with time-share operations.

➤**TOURIST INFORMATION: Los Cabos Tourism Board** (tel. 624/146–9628, www.visitcabo.com or www.visitloscabos.org). **Mexican Government Tourist & Promotion Board** (tel. 800/446–3942 from the U.S. and Canada,, www.visitmexico.com).

➤**GOVERNMENT ADVISORIES: U.S. Department of State** (Overseas Citizens Services Office, 2100 Pennsylvania Ave. NW, 4th fl., Washington, DC 20520, tel. 202/647–5225 interactive hotline or 888/407–4747, www.travel.state.gov). **Consular Affairs Bureau of Canada** (tel. 800/267–6788 or 613/944–6788, www.voyage.gc.ca). **U.K. Foreign and Commonwealth Office** (Travel Advice Unit, Consular Division, Old Admiralty Bldg., London SW1A 2PA, tel. 0870/606–0290 or 020/7008–1500, www.fco.gov.uk/travel). **Australian Department of Foreign Affairs and Trade** (tel. 300/139–281 travel advice, 02/6261–1299 Consular Travel Advice Faxback Service, www.dfat.gov.au). **New Zealand Ministry of Foreign Affairs and Trade** (tel. 04/439–8000, www.mft.govt.nz).

Web Sites

Do check out the World Wide Web when planning your trip. You'll find everything from weather forecasts to virtual tours of famous cities. Be sure to visit Fodors.com (www.fodors.com.), a complete travel-planning site. You can research prices and book plane tickets, hotel rooms, rental cars, vacation packages, and more. In addition, you can post your pressing questions in the Travel Talk section. Other planning tools include a currency converter and weather reports, and there are loads of links to travel resources.

The best information about ecotourism and environmental issues is at www.planeta.com. Discover Baja, a membership club for Baja travelers, has links and info at www.discoverbaja.com. Links to Los Cabos businesses and other information are available at www.bajalife.com, www.bajasites.com, www.baja-web.com, and www.loscabosguide.com.

When to Go

November through May are generally the driest months. During the peak of the rainy season (July through September), it may rain for a few hours daily. But the sun often shines for the rest of the day, and the off-season bargains may well compensate for the reduced tanning time. September and October usually see the most rain.

FORECASTS
Weather Channel (www.weather.com).

BAJA CALIFORNIA SUR

Jan.	73F	23C	May	91F	33C	Sept.	95F	35C
	54	12		59	15		73	23
Feb.	77F	25C	June	95F	35C	Oct.	91F	33C
	54	12		64	18		66	19
Mar.	80F	27C	July	97F	36C	Nov.	84F	29C
	54	12		71	22		66	16
Apr.	86F	30C	Aug.	97F	36C	Dec.	77F	25C
	55	13		73	23		54	12

index

FODOR'S POCKET LOS CABOS
EDITOR: Carolyn B. Heller

Editorial Production: David Downing

Editorial Contributors: Shannon Kelly, Maribeth Mellin

Maps: David Lindroth, *cartographer*; Rebecca Baer and Bob Blake, *map editors*

Design: Fabrizio La Rocca, *creative director*; Tigist Getachew, *art director*; Melanie Marin, *senior picture editor*

Production/Manufacturing: Robert B. Shields

Cover Photo (*Cabo San Lucas*): Robert Holmes/Corbis

COPYRIGHT

Third Edition

ISBN 1–4000–1402–6

ISSN 1531–3352

IMPORTANT TIP
Although all prices, opening times, and other details in this book are based on information supplied to us at press time, changes occur all the time in the travel world, and Fodor's cannot accept responsibility for facts that become outdated or for inadvertent errors or omissions. So **always confirm information when it matters**, especially if you're making a detour to visit a specific place. Your experiences—positive and negative—matter to us. If we have missed or misstated something, **please write to us.** We follow up on all suggestions. Contact the Pocket Los Cabos editor at editors@fodors.com or c/o Fodor's at 1745 Broadway, New York, New York 10019.

SPECIAL SALES
This book is available for special discounts for bulk purchases for sales promotions or premiums. Special editions, including personalized covers, excerpts of existing books, and corporate imprints, can be created in large quantities for special needs. For more information, write to Special Markets/Premium Sales, 1745 Broadway, MD 6-2, New York, New York 10019, or e-mail specialmarkets@randomhouse.com.

PRINTED IN THE UNITED STATES OF AMERICA

10 9 8 7 6 5 4 3 2 1